Getting a JOB

A Guide for Choosing a Career

Michael Pountney

InterVarsity Press
Downers Grove
Illinois 60515

InterVarsity Press is the book-publishing division of Inter-Varsity Christian Fellowship, a student movement active on campus at hundreds of universities, colleges and schools of nursing. For information about local and regional activities, write IVCF, 233 Langdon St., Madison, WI 53703.

Distributed in Canada through InterVarsity Press, 860 Denison St., Unit 3, Markham, Ontario L3R 4H1, Canada.

Acknowledgement is made to the following for permission to reprint copyrighted material:

Cover cartoon reprinted by permission: Tribune Company Syndicate, Inc.

Biblical quotations, unless otherwise noted, are taken from the Holy Bible: New International Version, *copyright © 1978 by the New York International Bible Society. Used by permission of Zondervan Bible Publishers.*

Bible references marked NEB are from The New English Bible. *© The Delegates of the Oxford University Press and The Syndics of the Cambridge University Press 1961, 1970. Reprinted by permission.*

Bible references marked RSV are from the Revised Standard Version of the Bible, copyrighted 1946, 1952, © 1971, 1973.

The cartoon and dialog on page 151 are taken from Doonesbury, Copyright, 1982, G. B. Trudeau. Reprinted with permission of Universal Press Syndicate. All rights reserved.

The appendix is taken from Life Planning *by Kirk E. Farnsworth and Wendell H. Lawhead. Revised edition © 1981 by Inter-Varsity Christian Fellowship of the United States of America. Used by permission of InterVarsity Press, Downers Grove, Illinois 60515.*

ISBN 0-87784-935-8

Printed in the United States of America

Library of Congress Cataloging in Publication Data
Pountney, Michael.
   Getting a job.

   Bibliography: p.
      1. Vocational guidance.   2. Christian life—1960-
I. Title.
HF5381.P678   1984   650.1'4   84-9039
ISBN 0-87784-935-8

19	18	7	16	15	14	13	12	11	10	9	8	7	6	5	4	3	2	1
99	98	97	96	95	94	93	92	91	90	89	88	87	86	85	84			

To Neil Graham and the British Columbia division of Canadian Inter-Varsity Christian Fellowship—my greatest boss and colleagues.

And to the eight UBC students whose insights and experiences are the seedthoughts of this book.

Introduction

The hollow laugh of cynicism is the dominant sound in final-year classes—cynicism, that is, about getting a job. Time after time in talking with seniors, I hear the same mournful question. Half bitter, half depressed, the students murmer, "Yeah, I'll get my degree, all right; but will I ever get a job?"

Christian students are not exempt from this vocational pressure. Prospective employers are rarely impressed by the mention on a résumé of Sunday-school leadership, campus Christian-organization presidency, or the habit of praying every day before breakfast. However, although they might not be exempt from anxiety or the conditions which cause anxiety, Christian students and Christian workers do have a considerable advantage when searching for employment. They have God.

At the University of British Columbia in Vancouver, Canada, I got to know a number of seniors in the Inter-Varsity Christian Fellowship chapter. (I worked for IVCF as university coordinator.) Observing their various methods and attitudes as they struggled with choosing careers and getting jobs triggered the idea that culminated in this book: Why not follow their methods of job seeking to

provide models for future Christian graduates—indeed, for all of us
Christians as we seek for or change our employment? If I could keep
track of their attempts to find work, using them like a control vari-
able in a sociological experiment, this material would provide helpful principles and examples for others in similar situations.

So I asked eight students, representing a cross-section of interests and personalities, if they would be willing to meet regularly
with me and my tape recorder to follow through, in discussion,
the actual ways in which they found their postgraduation jobs. I
realized a certain risk was involved. They might be unsuccessful.
They simply might not be able to start their careers or find employment that used their university training. They might not get jobs at
all; they might flunk out in their final year or fade into the background and become recluses in Rhodes.

Well, if that was to be so, then that would be the story I would
tell. I would fake nothing. Whether the students were heading for
failure or success, we decided to go ahead with the project and record the research. We believed that whatever the outcome for us as
individuals, God was with us and in us. And following him through
the final academic year into the world of work would be a high
Christian adventure and a tremendous learning experience, worthy
of being shared in a book.

Meet the Students
24 years old, 6' 1'', 180 lbs.: playing left wing on the IVCF hockey
team ... *Clark Stevens!*

Well, no, I don't suppose that will be too appropriate here. Let's
start again.

Rob Cousland: 23 years old. Majoring in religious studies. Failed
math in high school but still came second on the honor roll. Ex-
president of IVCF at UBC. Extremely literate, plays word games
with IVCF staff (and wins) and maintains a college average around
the As and Bs.

Carol George: 21 years old. Majoring in biology. Award-winning
junior-high student and a keen pianist. Her first year at university

made her work and study seriously for the first time. Especially good at sciences and math, maintains a B average, and doesn't feel she "does anything outstanding now."

Glenda Gilpin: 22 years old. Majoring in education. Top-notch student in elementary and high school, she entered a community college in the sciences and barely scraped through. Transferred to McGill University in Montreal, majored in English and finished with mostly As. Now doing the professional year at UBC to become an elementary teacher.

Steve Jenvy: 22 years old. Majoring in agriculture. Classical and jazz trombonist. Strong in math, weak in English. Originally in English at UBC, he transferred into agriculture when his father warned him English would leave no time for music. Has never received an A in his life (except for stage band) and usually struggles to get Bs. Dropped a course in his final year.

Herb Pond: 24 years old. Majoring in forestry. Married to Sandy (see below). One of four sons of an engineer; his mother climbed the Matterhorn while raising them. Went logging after high school for eight months; did first-year sciences at UBC, then forestry "clicked" for him. With time-outs for travel, work and marriage, Herb is in his seventh year since high school, final year at UBC, and still works full-time as a baggage handler for Canadian Pacific Airlines.

Sandy Pond: 23 years old. Majoring in forestry. Married to Herb (see above). Delightful junior-high student (she always got a B in French when I taught her), an energetic member of Christian school groups. Followed Herb into forestry after first year of sciences when she realized that forestry actually had openings for women.

Sheila Small: 22 years old. Majoring in psychology with a minor in philosophy. Did high school in Japan where she learned to work hard. Has found Canadian system pretty easy. Hates math, but does well in everything else. Spends summers guiding Japanese tourists around the Rockies.

And now, once again:

Clark Stevens: 24 years old. Majoring in psychology. Poor student in high school, just scraped through. Took two years off, traveling through Europe, Israel and India "searching for himself." In India he met and was strongly influenced by some Christian missionaries. Failed to get into Institute of Technology ("In retrospect, I'm glad of that"). Did one year at Bible College; then, via community college, came to UBC. Currently has high B average.

These are the eight students who graciously consented to meet with me during their final year and answer all the questions I fired at them about vocation. If any tributes are to be paid regarding the worth or value of this book, those tributes are theirs. Mine is the privilege of having known, admired, worked with and been influenced by these fine men and women of God.

This book is not a "how-to." It does not intend to give the reader six easy ways to get a good job and be a Christian at the same time. What it does contain are principles and examples, of and for followers of Jesus, about the whole process we call "getting a job."

When I Was a Child

I doubt whether young Frederic had many vocational doubts as he walked forward to the grand piano to give his first public concert. Even at eight, Chopin's career as a pianist and composer was already firmly set in his mind. I imagine the case was similar for young Ludwig, whose statue graces the instrument of little Schroeder in the Peanuts cartoon. He was casually given the baton on his teacher's absence at an orchestra rehearsal so that he, as a twelve-year-old, might conduct in the maestro's stead. When you have that kind of musical ability so early, such specific genius, you rarely hesitate over which career to choose.

I suspect the situation was different for you and me in our childhoods. While the occasional genius was already set in his or her career pattern before age ten, you and I were probably playing that typical childhood game of fantasy, "What Shall I Be When I Grow Up?" In our games we copied the sorts of jobs that we saw our adult heroes playing around us; the boys imitated truckers and police-car drivers, and the girls were teachers and nurses. This pattern of observation and imitation collected for us the raw data about the world of adult work. In a strange mixture of worship and envy of adults, we acted out our fantasies about growing up. I was always somewhat alarmed when my own two children would imitate their father preaching at a church service; the sight (and sound) of a six-year-old girl pleading with her sister, "You gotta believe," somehow unnerved me!

The problem for some of us is that we, or our overly ambitious or sentimental parents, interpreted our childhood play as "signs" that we were meant by destiny to evolve into successful career figures at the actual jobs we play-acted as children. Many an unfortunate boy has grown into adolescence with the job title "engineer" hung around his neck simply because he loved building dams in street gutters.

For some people, however, a genuine career direction has been set by a childhood incident. On the radio news this morning I heard the story of a sixteen-year-old coin collector and dealer who has already made a million dollars. This financial success story had its beginnings when a relative bought the boy a starter coin-collector kit at age nine. From the seeds of that childhood gift had sprung the tree of vocational success.

Such singlemindedness brings the taste of green envy to those of us who at twenty-five are still without a clue about what we want to do with our lives. The vision of top professionals who got their start through the gift of a Junior Brain Surgeon's Outfit (complete with stainless-steel knife, cut-away cerebellum and touch-up gray paint) or a Baby Beautician's Boutique is not without foundation. Career choices can be affected, even determined, by an apparently fortuitous gift or experience in childhood. Dr. Stephen Jay Gould, the still young but eminent paleontologist at Harvard University, told how he had early chosen his career:

First of all, I wanted to be a fireman or a policeman. But by the age of four or five I had opted for paleontology. That was because my father took me to visit the Museum of Natural History in New York. I found myself in front of a tyrannosaurus, dwarfed by its immense skeleton, when someone in the room sneezed. I thought that the sneeze came from the animal itself and I was terrified.

But later that day, I turned to my mother and announced my future career—paleontologist.[1]

Although none of the UBC students had experienced dramatic childhood events like this (or carried the specific genius of a Ludwig), several did remember having childhood ambitions. Sheila had wanted to be a writer, Rob a spy. Herb said, "My biggest childhood ambition was to be a jack-of-all-trades. I wanted to be able to do everything and do it well. I had visions of the guys who used to ride the rails from town to town during the depression and show up at a ranch and say, 'Have you got any work? I can do everything.' I wanted to be like that."

Steve amused us with his memory. "There were teachers all around us—my dad, my uncles. When my dad took out the strap at night, I knew he was the principal all right! When I was about ten or eleven I was going to be a dentist, partly because my dad's interested in teeth, very sensitive about teeth. Even to this day, you know, teeth are something—not my passion, but I do notice them."

Rob, on the other hand, was put off by his father's work environment, commenting, "When my father took me to the office, it was incredibly boring—I just couldn't wait to get out of there."

In one way or another, all of us have been affected by our exposures to vocation as children and young people—some to a greater degree, some to a lesser. I recall an uncle I admired a good deal as a child. He was a structural engineer. He took great interest in me for some reason, taking me to his office and an occasional site, giving me those fascinating engineers' diaries that small boys love, filled with delicious tables about the breaking point of steel girders and mathematical formulae for computing the volumes of cofferdams. When I added all this exposure to the fact that I belonged at my grammar school to the house named Dawnay (called so after a famous British engineer), I knew that destiny was shaping me for a career as an engineer. It was, as you might suspect, a short-lived piece of guidance, which I had dismissed by the time I was thirteen.

Pressure to Conform and Continue

Another way our upbringing may affect our career choices is in the occupational history of our families. What family traditions suggest that we ought to follow in a certain type of work? Steve mentioned that he was surrounded by teachers as he was growing up. Herb talked of the ties he felt with his lumberjack grandfather. Were there pressures on these students to follow in the family footsteps?

Has your family had the same ancestral business since your forefathers stepped off the Mayflower? Is your father's ambition, mentioned repeatedly, the addition of "and sons" (perhaps he's progressive: let's add "and daughters") on the painted sign in his office window or over the corner store? Has your mother been preening you for law school ever since you won your first argument over the porridge when you were three? No doubt for some students these family expectations, pressures perhaps, are strong; and whether they are covert or overt, they are a factor to be reckoned with when analyzing the reasons for a particular career choice.

As a group, the UBC students were delightfully free from parental pressures to conform to any particular career expectation. Only a couple felt that their parents had laid ambitions on them. Herb admitted he had been pressured to become a lawyer, and Sandy had to fight off the expectation that she would follow a myriad of uncles and aunts to a certain Bible school in Saskatchewan.

"What affected me as a child," said Carol, "was the whole work ethic, the expectation that whatever I'd do, I should put my all into it."

Sheila, the daughter of missionaries, admitted, "I felt no expectation from my family, but I felt the expectation from within myself —that within three or four years I should be, not necessarily a missionary, but certainly in full-time Christian work. But I was never pressured."

Of course, expectations and duties can be unconsciously created. Although a parent might never articulate an ambition for a child to follow a certain pattern, that ambition may be suggested in numerous ways.

As you take vocational stock of yourself, planning and preparing for a career, try exploring your childhood and family background to determine the pressures and attitudes that, in part, have formed you. An interesting, helpful way to do this is to talk with your parents about your childhood, asking them to remember how they perceived you as a growing child, what characteristics and ambitions they saw in you, what skills and attitudes of vocational significance they noticed.

An evening spent this way could yield some valuable insights into yourself. But besides that it could bring a new closeness and understanding into your relationship. It lets your parents know that you take their opinions and memories seriously; and if you think their opinions are important, it means that you think *they* are important. That's what will be communicated. Besides, parents love to reminisce about their children. They might even bring out the colored slides and home movies. Through the eyes of their memory you may be able to see yourself "as others see you."

A recent Mother's Day article in a city newspaper looked at this parent-child vocational link from a different perspective, but a very positive one. The Montreal *Gazette* examined what could be a modern trend, "Mother serving as example for the offspring in a capacity other than cook, dishwasher, bed maker and dispenser of tender loving care." There followed interviews with both men and women who had definitely chosen to follow in their mothers' career footsteps. A son had left law to become a doctor, "like his mother"; others had become colleagues and partners with their mothers in broadcasting, design, dance and modeling. If such role copying is indeed becoming a trend, it could be a happy one for parent-offspring relationships.[2]

Momma Don't Allow No Trumpet Playing 'Round Here!

Problems arise when the future that the parents desire for their children conflicts with what the children themselves want. I met this dilemma in a unique and accentuated form with international students who came to Vancouver to study with a view to returning to a highly defined occupational and familial role at home, where social and community norms prevailed. These students found that Canada opened up for them a totally new set of possibilities; they felt the urge to escape from the limiting expectations of their homeland so that they could be independent in their career choices. But such independence carried an enormous price tag for some of them. To choose a career outside the roles of parental expectation might mean a final exclusion from all privileges of family, inheritance and religion.

I sympathize with both sides in such a conflict. I am a parent. I do have ambitions for my children and can appreciate that other parents do too. I understand what it must be like to have built up a business all your life with the sole intention of handing it over to your eldest as a shining success, the gift of a lifetime—literally. And I can understand the hurt that there would be if such a son or daughter refused to accept the gift—was totally uninterested, or declared himself or herself far too superior to take on the lowly task of the business, or adopted a career that was opposed to all the values that I as a parent stood for.

But I can see, too, the yearning for freedom and independence in the choice of work that a young man or woman has, indeed must have, for this is the correct and basic pattern for growth into adulthood. I see nothing but disaster ahead for the young people who allow themselves to be bought, bribed or bullied into a family vocational mold which patently does not fit. However, as with all conflict, nothing is resolved through sudden departures in the night, open rebellion or abuse. Conflicts of this sort, if they are to be resolved at all (and occasionally they cannot be), are resolved through discussion, prayer, openness to understanding the other's viewpoint, and compromise.

Joseph and Sons—Carpenters

I wonder if Jesus ever felt any vocational pressures from his earthly father to stay in the family carpentry business for a little longer— say, till he was thirty-five or forty, when as the eldest son he might have become a family partner or owner. How did Simon Peter's father respond when he learned that his son wouldn't be around to help him anymore but had gone off with some itinerant evangelist? And what did Matthew's mother say when he returned home and told her he was going to quit the tax business? "But think of the security you're giving up, my boy, that steady income! And who's going to look after your poor old Momma now?"

We have, of course, no direct information about these conjectural questions, but vocational and parental conflicts were not completely unknown in first-century Judea. In Luke 2:49 we have a clue, a piece of foreshadowing, about the problems Jesus and his family were going to face with respect to vocation, loyalty and expectations. There is, in this visit to Jerusalem, already an awareness that Jesus was operating with two sets of loyalties, an immediate one to an immediate and earthly father, and a superior one to his heavenly Father. Even for Jesus Christ these two sets of values could collide; eighteen years after this incident Jesus left the family business —and the family—for good.

For his followers, too, the call to discipleship could cut diagonally across family work ties. If we presume that Paul's father had aspirations for his son's brilliant legal career, what a downfall to see him an unemployed religious fanatic or, at best, a tentmaker! At least four of Jesus' original twelve had to leave family fishing operations. Simon the Zealot's family (although being a Zealot wasn't exactly a paid political office) probably never imagined the vocational setup that he was getting into when he left politics.

What does this suggest, then, for you and me as we seek to follow the Father's call to involve ourselves in his vocation? The call to follow Jesus often adds a dimension of tension to career plans. Christian students do not find it easy to explain to their nonbelieving parents why they are choosing a certain path. As Jesus and his disciples (and many a Christian man and woman since) had to leave hearth and home, and family business, so might you and I. We, too, have a higher loyalty to a heavenly Father. The tough words of Jesus in Matthew 10:34-39 might be relevant to those who are faced with

an out-and-out conflict between what they feel led to do as Christians and what their family is trying to persuade them to do:
Do not suppose that I have come to bring peace to the earth. I did not come to bring peace, but a sword. For I have come to turn [here he quotes the Old Testament prophet Micah]
   "a man against his father,
   a daughter against her mother,
   a daughter-in-law against her mother-in-law—
   a man's enemies will be the members of his own household."
Anyone who loves his father or mother more than me is not worthy of me; anyone who loves his son or daughter more than me is not worthy of me; and anyone who does not take his cross and follow me is not worthy of me. Whoever finds his life will lose it, and whoever loses his life for my sake will find it.

Set in a chapter that narrates the sending out of the Twelve in a style reminiscent of prophetic and apocalyptic literature, the language is clearly, to my mind, hyperbolic. By heightening contrasts and pushing possibilities to extremes, Jesus is emphasizing the great truth that he is of such importance that he must be above and beyond all human loves; that, if it should ever come to a stark choice, *he* must be chosen above all human relationships. The words tell us, too, that on occasion a Christian's spiritual enemies will be from his own household. In William Barclay's words, Jesus offers warfare and a choice, "and the bitterest thing about this warfare was that a man's foes would be those of his own household."[3]

This is no text to use against family love, mind you, as if Jesus were actively sowing hatred. Jesus is not saying that family love is wrong, that it should be avoided or annulled by a believer. He is saying, though, that when it comes to the crunch, the showdown, the disciple who is to be worthy of Christ is to choose Christ above his own family. If a young Christian is being pressured into a career that is patently unchristian—like a family casino business or a family construction company founded on kickbacks and shoddy workmanship—these words of Jesus give us clear directions about the choice to be made. In such a case, vocational guidance is reduced to ethical and spiritual terms: "Follow me."

Much more subtle, and therefore more difficult, would be the case in which a student is pressured by family into a vocation that is inherently good but which the student feels is not the call of Christ for him. The student, loving both family and Christ, feels the tension of the twin loyalties which are not to be resolved through a simple ethical choice of good versus bad. What can a person do in that situation?

First, he or she must come to a conviction as to the call of Christ, and this comes through prayer, counsel and Scripture. Proceeding from the clarity of that conviction, the student must carefully explain to the parents, even while acknowledging the possibility of hurt and disappointment, how he or she perceives the career choice. The parents will gain an understanding of what motivates the student and will appreciate both his strength of conviction and his sensitivity about a decision so potentially divisive.

I am fully convinced that the career decision must be made by the young person who is to enter the career, and that such a decision must be made freely and courageously. We are to make our own decisions, and we are to own them thereafter. That is maturity.

After You Graduate

It was Careers Day at my high school. We boys lined up for nearly an hour outside a classroom, knowing that within sat a special person who knew all about "careers." My turn came at last.

"Well, son," the interviewer began, "have you decided what you want to be when you leave school?"

"Yes, sir."

"Good. What is it?"

"I want to be a captain in the Royal Navy."

"Oh, well, er ... good. Next!"

The whole thing took forty-six seconds. So ended my one and only careers interview.

Teen-age Optimism

Although many high schools tout their emphasis on career guidance, little of worth seems to be happening. Our UBC students talked of their own high-school days with less than enthusiasm. None had received any consistent or effective vocational counseling. They did remember, however, their idealism about their futures. Stated Rob, "We were idealistic about our potential. We knew we were capable of whatever we decided to do. We just chose courses to keep open as many options as possible."

Sheila continued in a similar vein, "I've always been idealistic, and I certainly was in junior high . . . about everything. I thought I could really do anything I wanted—be a professional musician, professional athlete—anything. No problem."

Carol had less idealism but a greater awareness of her teachers' and friends' expectations. "In high school I was highly involved in music, and a lot of people expected me to want to go on in that. But I knew that I really didn't want to."

Most of us knew that lurking in the background somewhere was the thought of employment and that our course choices at junior and senior high would affect later options. We knew, too (or thought we knew, and would have been astounded and indignant if told otherwise), that good results in school meant the first steps on the high road to success, fame and fortune.

But what if high school was less than successful? What about the Peppermint Patties of this world for whom "nothing but D-minuses lurk outside"? Clark left high school with little accomplishment behind him. "I was a pretty poor student. Just getting through high school was an achievement for me. I wasn't really thinking career at all. I was kind of antifamily, antiestablishment, anticareer, anti-everything."

Clark took two years off after leaving high school, traveling around the world, searching for himself. After a one-year stretch at a Bible school in Oregon, he got back into the academic stream by registering at a community college. For students like Clark, just being present in class those first days marks a sort of triumph; they've successfully made the transition back into formal education. Often a maturity of mind and breadth of outlook are the hallmark of such students.

As you reflect on your own high-school days and the ways in which they have opened or narrowed your vocational options, take heart. Dropped courses, bad grades and missed subjects are not irredeemable. Through retraining, high school, mature-student scholarships and so forth, it is fairly easy to retrace your steps or even gain a high-school diploma if needed. You *can* return down the academic track a mile or two further to catch a train you previously missed.

The years between high school and university entrance are a time of self-searching for many young people. Some are attracted more to the idea of travel or work than to a direct continuation of formal education. I left high school at fifteen to become a navigator, more fascinated by the sea than by studies. Those years of late-teen travel and work gave me excellent experiences and made me come to grips with who I was as a person and as a Christian. They provided me with challenges that formed my faith; I saw the kingdom of darkness at firsthand and resolved to choose the kingdom of light. That, I think, is a more important task than choosing the right job or "getting on."

But let's move on now, leaving high school behind and taking a look at that first year in college.

On the College Track—and Changing Trains
Students in an average freshman class are like travelers in a mainline railway station. Some are there with purpose and motivation. They know which train they're getting and from which platform it leaves. Their baggage is neatly packed at their feet; their ticket is in their hand; they know their destination and destiny. Others, frankly, are not so certain. They're still searching the timetable boards, tossing coins, debating destinations, unsure about everything. Still others have actually missed their intended train and, unsure as to their next step, are sleeping listlessly in the waiting room, at least warm and dry. First-year students, with three or four years of planning to catch their vocational trains, come in a dazzling variety of styles and are faced with a dazzling variety of choices.

Carol was one who arrived on campus knowing which major she wanted but knowing also that her choice would surprise her family. "When I told people that I was going into biology at university, they flipped and thought I was crazy. Everybody said I should do music." It's good to arrive knowing beforehand what you want to do and having the independence to make up your own mind. Those who can cheerfully swim against the current of assumptions are fortunate. They have a strong sense of what they want. They are firm enough to survive the expressions of amazement, even contempt, which come their way. That kind of certainty can pay off in terms of building a career foundation early in university life.

Others, though having obvious gifts and strengths that would lead toward a particular vocation, have had the foresight to look ahead, assess the total life situation of that career, reject it and choose an alternative. Steve explains his rejection of music as a career: "Why not choose music? I guess I didn't want to do what I could see my band teacher doing. What I thought I could be—a sort of glorious jazz musician or freelancer—well, first of all I knew the difficulty in achieving that, and second I realized that it wasn't quite the lifestyle I could enjoy."

It is never too late to make a change in your major or even in the degree itself. What you might lose in years (those ephemeral things that seem so long from the front and so short from the back), you most certainly gain in happiness and freedom.

My friend Laura has just entered a new field at McGill University. Facing her third and final year in engineering, she eventually faced up to a fact that had been knocking at her consciousness for some months. She no longer even liked engineering; she wanted out! So she plucked up her courage, sought out advisers and faculty heads, ignored the scorn of unsympathetic friends, and transferred into translation in the department of linguistics. What she has breathed so far in these first weeks is nothing but the pure air of freedom. She has happiness about her vocation that has been lacking for a long time.

For Laura, graduation will be delayed a year or two. But there comes a time for all students (well—nearly all) when studies are over, classes are completed and it is time to graduate. The future has arrived.

Facing the Future with Confidence

The university can be a cocoon. Wrapped in the silken security of continuous course selection, hanging onto the thin but strong threads of student loans and part-time work, fed with the fellowship of a student Christian group, that cocoon can be very attractive. We all know a grad student who is basically in school because he is too fearful of the outside world to leave the womb of campus.

Graduation, like one of Gail Sheehy's "passages," is a rite that is typically ambiguous. It brings apprehension and excitement, fear and delight. Our UBC students felt both sides of the emotional tension, but were predominantly confident about themselves, their futures and their God.

"I'm by no means depressed," said Clark. "I do look forward to getting out so I can finally get some training. I've had enough education."

Carol commented similarly, "I'm really looking forward to getting out, into the world kind of thing. I'm starting to feel a lot more confident, a lot more optimistic, about all the possibilities that I can take in."

At the same time, though, this optimistic desire to "get out" and enter the world of work can be tinged with anxiety. Clark admitted to feeling "a little insecure" and others confessed their inability to see much beyond the next four or five years. As the students attempted to project their lives into the distant future, their uneasiness increased. They felt simultaneously "O.K.—but not O.K."

Even in the Middle Ages, debt and uncertainty could plague a graduate's future. Read the lament of Master David, who traveled from London to study and graduate from the University of Bologna in the 1170s:

I am unable to leave Bologna because of a mountain of debt that weighs me down and destroys my substance. So far as I can reckon, ninety pounds would scarcely suffice to clear the principal that I have borrowed, not counting the interest of two and a half years. No month passes without my having to raise another twenty-one shillings for my debts. I had hoped for a better

income, . . . and this expectation has led me to spend more and
stay in Bologna longer than I could afford. This is always the way
things happen.[1]

And you thought paying back student loans was a twentieth-century problem!

For people of my generation, those born during the Second
World War, the opportunities that careers held in terms of satisfaction, success and advancement seemed limitless. We faced the future with utter confidence. I went through adolescence believing
that I could virtually choose any career I wished. Because of the
booming economy of the postwar years, the expansion of educational and social services, the democratization of routes into the
good jobs, and the reduction of occupational privilege, this attainability was true.

Therefore, people of my age tend to have surpassed the success
levels of their parents. You can readily check this with a little research among your friends' parents. I did and found a stable boy's
son who is now a chief auditor for an oil company, a small-town
farmer's son who is vice president of a pipeline company, and a
corner-store proprietor's daughter who is now a doctor.

However, the question hanging over the heads of today's students
is this: will they, too, be able to attain similar success in their careers?
Will they be able to surpass their fathers' and mothers' levels of
success? Several factors suggest that the answer might be no.

The Bad News

An article in *Saturday Night* entitled "Life among the Boomies"
has some hard things to say to students who are graduating in the
early eighties.[2] The Boomies are the children of the postwar baby
boom, let's say children who were born between 1950 and the early
1960s. They number about six million in Canada alone. Children
born earlier faced a growing and developing job market as they
graduated and searched for employment. Even if every other option
fell through, they could always get a job in government or teaching. But not so for the Boomies.

Those forming the latter half of the baby boom and those coming after it will enter an employment arena that is vastly different from the market of fifteen years ago. The article points out some of those differences:

1. There are just too many highly educated university graduates looking for managerial or executive positions in these economically uncertain days.

2. Children born after 1952 have a twenty-five per cent less chance of being promoted to middle management than do children born before 1952. "There is a split between the two groups: the pre-Boomies and early Boomies, who more or less had the way opened up for them in the management of corporations; and the late Boomies, who hope only to find a reasonably secure and well-paid place somewhere in the bowels of the corporations."

3. Expectations have to come down. The scope and success of the postwar world of high employment (Choose your job! Choose where you want to live! Choose how high you want to climb!) are not going to be repeated. "The kids today are not going to get the income or the jobs that the students of ten years ago did. I try to tell people that the 1950's or 1960's were unique in Canada. The jobs and the incomes that the kids got then were just *unheard* of. And now we're back to a normal period of our history. Expectations have to come down."

4. Job security will be increasingly tenuous and fragile.

5. Increasingly, today's employees will regard their work as "just a job" and look for their fulfillment elsewhere. "The organization-man has been replaced by the employee who openly declares that his job is only his *job,* and that his real interest lies in canoeing or biofeedback."

6. The growing severity of competition for the top jobs is inescapable.

The major point is clear. Young people graduating today will have a much more restricted vocational opportunity than their predecessors. That means fewer jobs, greater scrambling and competition, more unemployment and a standard of living probably lower than expected. Many students reading this book will be unable to achieve as high a standard of living as their parents.

Two further points from the article are worth mentioning. Married Boomies will, in all probability, have to have both spouses working full-time for a long time if they want to enter the materially full life of the average North American consumer. The major financial burden facing a married couple will be to afford a house. These hard facts are some of the reasons why Boomies are turning away from studies in the arts and pure sciences to enroll in business administration and computer science—courses that relate closely to the actual tasks and rewards of today's marketplace. (In 1982 nearly half of all bachelor degrees awarded in the United States were in strictly occupational fields like business and engineering, and enrollment in the liberal arts had dropped to a low of seven per cent, one-third of what it was fifteen years ago.)[3]

Many other prophecies of doom exist, not only in popular literature but also in academic treatises. Paul Vitz in *Psychology as Religion* predicts that the large wave of rising expectations about career success is headed for a breakup in the coming decade.[4] He makes the following eight unhappy observations.

1. Today's graduates have an unrealistically high expectation of vocational success.

2. Economic growth in the United States has slowed considerably and is not likely to match that of the last thirty years.

3. Career dissatisfaction regularly strikes people in their late thirties and forties, but today's graduates are likely to have less freedom and fewer choices when it comes time to cope with that.

4. Many of today's popular careers, such as teaching, psychology, medicine and law, are already overcrowded. Future access to these fields is likely to be restricted.

5. A high proportion of today's career opportunities are in large organizations or bureaucracies. Such megaliths tend to limit opportunities for individual advancement and destroy chances for effective, gratifying work.

6. Many graduates have no emotional or family ties to provide an

alternative source of meaning and support; and vocational pressures often cause existing ties to crumble, leaving careerists lonely
and accentuating their isolation.

7. Many graduates will be choosing careers simply because it was
all they could get; fewer will pursue vocational goals out of commitment or interest.

8. Most important, careers are intrinsically too weak to carry the
huge psychic burden they are now given. Even among that small
group who do succeed, many find success unsatisfying, even bleak
and empty.

These are indeed tough words, and they paint a gray picture of
your future. I would understand completely if you threw this book
in the air in despair and bought a ticket to Bermuda. You may as
well be warm while unemployed!

What can a person about to enter the career stage of life do in
the face of such a gloomy scenario? Is there an alternative to despair?

Finding Perspective
Traditionally, a person's career was the most significant area of life.
It was a possession to be displayed, a vehicle for social and personal
advancement. You could escape an impoverished or lower class
background by success in an established field of work, preferably a
profession. An unhappy marriage, an unhealthy body, a character
weakness, a disappointing offspring, an inner emptiness of soul—
all these could be mastered or ignored as long as the major structure of career, of advancement and promotion, of esteem and hon-
or, held firm. The significance of a good career was that it carried
your identity. The job made you; you were your job. The first question people asked you in any social gathering was invariably, "What
do you do for a living?" And your answer was your identity card into
privilege and acceptance or scorn and rejection.

A young girl from a country village in the west of England won a
scholarship to an exclusive, private girls' school. On her first day,
another girl asked her about her father's occupation. "He's a

butcher," she replied, only to be immediately aware of the other girl's disdain. The next time she was asked, she replied, "He's a Master butcher" (as indeed he was). But the displeasure was still there. Soon she learned the correct answer. "My father is a self-employed businessman," she would say, to the approval of her questioners.

The myth that makes your job title synonymous with success and satisfaction has been in circulation for decades. Millions have believed it and believe it still. But it is not true. Of all people, Christians know that their identity, satisfaction and fulfillment are not simply the end products of their careers. We are *not* our jobs. Although the temptations to accept the old myth are still very strong, Christians understand, as J. I. Packer reminds us in *Knowing God,* that our major purpose in life is to know God![5] We are human beings created in the marvelous image of God, finding both our identity and our fulfillment in our relationship with him. For it is God, not the fringe-benefit package from Gulf Oil, who "crowns me with love and compassion [and] satisfies my desires with good things" (Ps 103:4-5). Our status comes from being brought into a right relationship with God through Jesus Christ, not from the dimensions of our office desk and the impressiveness of our job title.

The modern view of careers, the myth of personal status through occupational advancement, has not only usurped God, it has also made career a substitute for other areas of life where fulfillment was historically found. I am referring to the satisfaction that comes from stable family love, permanent relationships of fidelity, and good friendships. In this age of instant marital breakdown, temporary sexual liaisons, and pervasive loneliness, some men and women cling grimly to their careers as their only hope for inner peace and wholeness. What a forlorn hope! No career is big enough to provide the inner satisfaction that love was designed to produce, or replace the essential fulfillment that comes from divine and human relationships.

Not by Bread Alone
Materialism is another success that doesn't satisfy. Measuring suc-

cess by materialistic standards, by salary, fringe benefits and bonuses, leads us off into a second false search for satisfaction. The prophet Jeremiah knew not only that the boast of wealth was a false virtue but that it was not a virtue at all. "Let not . . . the rich man boast of his riches, but let him who boasts boast about this: that he understands and knows me, that I am the LORD" (Jer 9:23-24).

Unfortunately, the futility of satisfaction via wealth often hits us only after the fact. It is well illustrated, for example, by the middle-aged syndrome of "I've got everything I want but I'm still empty inside." I heard these very words recently from a professional hockey player who was giving a testimony at one of our youth meetings. That awareness of materialistic completeness but inner emptiness motivated his search for God. Perhaps this is why some rich, apparently successful forty-year-old men do the craziest things, like leaving their families and running off with twenty-year-old secretaries, or taking up soft drugs, or searching Katmandu for their personal Swami.

Christians know that materialistic success, through career or any other way, is not to be a primary ambition. The Bible teaches clearly that the hollow lure of gold leads to emptiness, selfishness and a peculiarly metallic deadness of heart. Jesus warns the person set on career-seeking for money, "Where your treasure is, there your heart will be also" (Mt 6:21). This is both a warning against materialistic ambition and a prophecy of what will happen if the warning is disobeyed. If, like Eustace in *The Voyage of the Dawn Treader*, you think dragonish thoughts, you will turn into a dragon. "Sleeping on a dragon's hoard, with greedy dragonish thoughts in his heart, Eustace had become a dragon himself."[6] C. S. Lewis and Jesus said the same thing. If your treasure is money, your heart will turn dead with greed. You turn into what you lust after.

It is inherently foolish for Christians to set their hearts on money and then look to a certain career to provide it. That is confusing materialistic success with real fulfillment. The primary reason for entering any career must not be lucrative gain.

Neither must we look to a career to find that deep inner satisfaction that can only come from accepting the lordship of Jesus Christ over our lives and living in his Spirit. The great apostle Paul knew the secret of inner satisfaction. He wrote to his friends in Philippi, "I have learned to be content whatever the circumstances. I know what it is to be in need, and I know what it is to have plenty. I have learned the secret of being content in any and every situation, whether well fed or hungry, whether living in plenty or in want. I can do everything through him who gives me strength" (Phil 4: 11-13).

"Un Bon Job, Un Bon Boss"

Where I live in Montreal this bilingual phrase has become almost a proverb. It is used for two reasons: first, to illustrate how French-Canadians have assimilated so many English words into their language, and, second, because it sums up the basic aspirations of so many Montrealers. All anyone wants is a good job with a good boss.

I believe that in spite of all the gloomy predictions, most of us will be able to gain pleasure from our work. Although ultimate pleasure comes from God, there is nevertheless a pleasure and an accomplishment that come from doing a good job well. New and worthwhile jobs are being created all the time. Working conditions are, in the main, improving steadily. Many of the older, monotonous, routine tasks are being eliminated. Capable, energetic, well-qualified graduates are finding interesting positions. There will always be room for creativity and innovation. There will always be challenges to face and overcome. There still is hope that you will find a job to bring its own appropriate satisfaction. You are not doomed to be a hamburger clerk at McDonalds forever.

Overarching the whole world of work and career and your place in that world is the grace and favor of God. With such a resource, Christian graduates looking for a career can search optimistically and patiently. Surely we can trust ourselves to his love and care, believing that he who is Creator, the very author of work, can lead us in our search for work so that we find pleasure and joy.

Circling Around

Imagine. You're at the back of the line-up at the world-famous Gertie's Smorgasbord. Slowly you shuffle forward, mouth watering in anticipation. At last you make it to the counters, and there they are—dozens and dozens of succulent dishes laid out for you at your lip-tips.

You are momentarily paralyzed by indecision, overwhelmed by the staggering variety of choices. That moment of indecision lengthens into minutes. You can't even decide which soup to start with . . . asparagus, mushroom, cream of celery, tomato, beef 'n barley, turnip. Turnip?

Your indecision is making you miserable, actually panic-stricken, as you realize that the people behind you apparently suffer no such uncertainty. They overtake you, quickly choosing, relentlessly emptying each dish before your eyes. You realize with horror that your own failure to choose when you had the opportunity has diminished your chances of selecting the best meal. Blindly and thoughtlessly, you lunge to fill your plate, but even as you do so the chefs are clearing off the remaining dishes and closing down the counter. Gertie's has got you!

Choosing a career can be a little like that. Even a cursory glance at *The Dictionary of Occupational Titles* shows us a bewildering array of careers. And just beginning to make those "narrowing down" decisions can be difficult, even paralyzing, especially as you see other friends happily overtaking you with their crisp decisiveness. Hanging over your head like a spectrum is the nightmare of letting the choice go too long—of having the choices severely curtailed by the time you have made up your mind, of losing out to someone else who thought and acted more quickly.

Circles of Vocation

A simple technique can help you narrow down your vocational choices. The "circle of vocation" principle is a visual design idea by which you can begin on paper to zero in on a vocational zone. We start by deciding on the biggest possible job category that interests you (say, engineering, or working with animals). Then we slowly limit that large-circle vocational zone by drawing smaller circles which represent a narrowing down of that initial category.

In order to come up with these categories and subcategories, you will need some accurate and up-to-date careers information. You can get this easily by visiting the library and checking through the reference material under the heading *Vocations*. A fine index of vocational resources is also provided in the appendixes of the careers workbook *Life Planning*.[1]

If you already know the broad category of career that interests you, drop a letter to some companies or professional associations involved and beg for a contact. A personal visit to an office or a guided tour of a plant is immensely useful in getting a sense of what kinds of jobs are available in a particular industry or career.

Having now some idea of what's out there, you are ready to think about yourself: what in that vast array is right for you?

Let's imagine how this idea of a "circle of vocation" will work as we have an imaginary conversation together.

You: You know, I'm going to be graduating eventually and I've got to start choosing a career. But I haven't got a clue as to what sort of a job to look for. I don't even know what I can do, could do, or even want to do.

Me: Have you read Mike Pountney's book on vocation? No, seriously . . . let's talk and see if we can begin to get a handle on the sorts of jobs that might interest you and that you'd be good at. I call this drawing the circles of vocation. What I'm trying to do is lead you from the broadest, vaguest feelings that you might be interested in, say, computers, through a process of narrowing down ideas until we arrive at something more focused, like being involved in the selling of some of the newest microchip hardware.

You: Well, I doubt if it will work, but let's give it a go.

Me: I'm glad you said that or I'd have to rewrite all this. Now. Thinking in as big a category as possible, what sort of area are you interested in? What's the occupational zone we can start with?

You: Actually it's easier to tell you what I'm not interested in than the other way round.

Me: O.K. Start with that.

You: Well, I don't want to work with people. I don't want to teach or be a social worker or become a missionary in darkest New York or work for a well-known campus Christian group or anything like that. I think I want to work with things.

Me: What sorts of things?

You: Things that move. I've always loved trains, buses, planes, ships, anything that went from one place to another. Anything that could move.

Me: Right. We can start with that. I'll draw a huge circle and label it "Transportation," understanding that this includes "anything that moves," counting both people movers and merchandise movers. (See figure 1.)

You: What do we do now?

Me: Now we've got to zoom in a bit and make it smaller. Couple of ways we could do this, actually. By cargo: people or things? Then what sort of things? Or by method: what do you think you're most interested in working with, taxis or tanks? Maybe you should join the army?

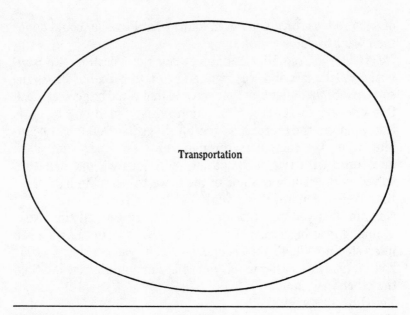

Transportation

Figure 1.

You: No, thanks . . . or should I say, No tanks!

Me: Another way to begin narrowing down is to think of what work you'd actually like to do with these things that move. Do you want to drive or fix? Do you want to be in the cockpit or in the pits?

You: Well, I'm no mechanic. I don't want to build them or fix them or oil them or anything like that. I'll tell you what I like doing. I like playing with schedules. I used to love (still do!) trying to arrange a train journey from one end of the country to the other— picking up all the right connections, planning the fastest routes with the best timing. That sort of thing is really more fun in Europe than in Canada or the States. When I went to Europe last year I bought a Eurail Pass and a copy of the Cooks International Time-table. Best fun I ever had was before we'd even left. I worked out how to ride the trains from Dieppe to Athens going through as many countries as possible. It was fabulous. And we only missed one connection, at Avignon, when the TEE train . . . oh, well, I'll tell you about that when you've got this chapter finished.

Me: Thanks. I can hardly wait. Now I don't suppose we can really build a career on leafing through Cooks Timetable, but we have got something here that we can use. So I'll draw a smaller circle and label it "Administration and Scheduling." (See figure 2.)

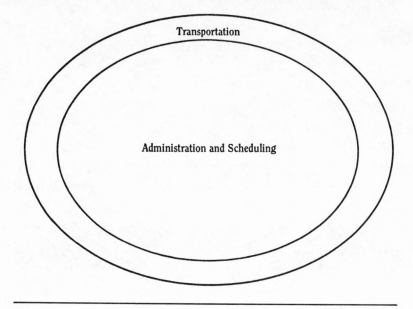

Figure 2.

Now, where to from here? It seems to me that you need to decide what sort of level to aim at. You could work as a dispatcher, for instance, for a taxi firm or trucking company. You could get into air traffic control if you want to be a precise and exact controller of things. Or you could become chief of operations for Air Canada or TWA.

You: Well, I don't think I want to do permanent night shift, sending taxis to pick up late-night travelers. Though I did do that sort of thing for an ambulance company in Toronto for a summer. That wasn't too bad. But I wouldn't want to stick there all my life. Besides, how do I get to use my great university training telling a cab to go to Yonge and Bay for a stranded shopper? I'd like to be in charge, to manage something eventually. I'd like to be responsible for planning things, perhaps a bus system for a new town or a schedule for a subway operation.

Me: O.K. Another circle, with "Planning or Schedules Manage-

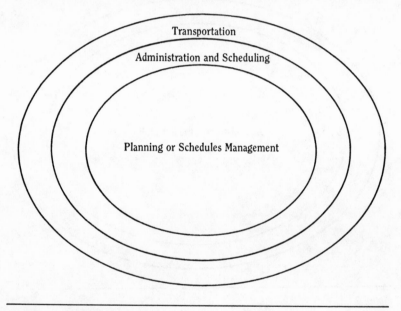

Figure 3.

ment" as its label. (See figure 3.)

You: Now I can see how this is beginning to work . . . a little, that is. It's a bit like a movie camera zooming in and cutting down the size of the picture.

Me: Right, exactly; you took the words cut of my mouth.

You: Not surprising; they're your words.

Me: To continue. Now I think we need a smaller circle still, one that is going to be a clue as to where we can start sending off a few letters. Who do you want to work for? Want to work with buses and rush-hour schedules for a city system? Want to be a professional people-mover in urban planning? Want to control the skies over O'Hare airport?

You: No. None of those. I know planes are exciting and modern and all that, and there's no limit to what they're going to do in the sky over the next century, but I'll keep my feet on the ground. On track, you might say. I'll do something with trains. In spite of Boeing, they've still got a great future.

Me: So that leaves us with an inner circle labeled "Trains . . . Via Rail or Amtrak." I added Amtrak in case you want to emigrate. Come to think of it, we could put in "Ethiopian National Railways." In fact, I've got a friend who did a Ph.D. on the railway system in Southeast Asia. He hasn't got a job yet either.

You: Thanks.

Me: Now, I haven't the foggiest notion about how you become a schedules manager with Via Rail, but let's suggest what you can do next. Write to all the people you can think of who are in the train business, perhaps even some in other countries too. Tell them your career interests and see what happens. Let them know any special experience you've had in transportation, and give them a résumé of your education. Incidentally, got any useful courses in there, say, Trains 202 or Timetables 313?

You: Dozens of them. Got an A in Wheels 415 and the seminar on Signals. No, seriously, I've got some good math, my sociology ought to be useful, and I'm doing a course in business management right now.

Me: O.K. Let's draw our last circle. But before we do, let me make a comment. There are undoubtedly very few jobs—perhaps even none—in transcontinental railways these days. That's partly because of mismanagement and budget cuts, and partly because air transportation has simply taken over the market. In Canada, I know, Via Rail is a mess, a sort of poor man's political football that nobody wants anymore. So to be considering a career in trains, no matter how much they thrill you, is not a prime example of sensible future planning. It will probably make more sense to check out a future in large city and suburban commuter traffic, like San Francisco's BART, or to look underground and explore the world's metro systems. They're still building subways. (See figure 4.)

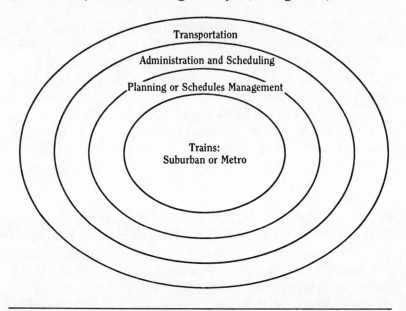

Figure 4.

Serving God in a Real Way

That's how it works. It's a simple idea, but it may help. You can at least get a handle on the choosing process and gain the psychological comfort of having written something down in black and white.

One more example might be useful. Imagine that you are a counselor at college and a young Christian enters, anxious about the whole area of deciding what she wants to do. When you ask that first penetrating question ("Hey, what d'you wanna do when you grow up?"), all her strong sense of commitment will allow her to reply is that she wants to serve God in a "real way." You realize intuitively that what she means by *real* is going to be crucial! Out come your pen and paper and on goes the first circle—serving God (see figure 5).

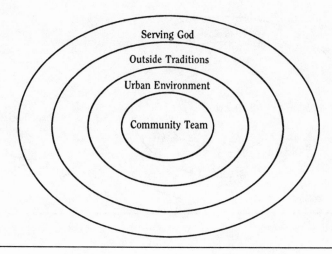

Figure 5.

Further discussion tells you that by "serving God in a real way" she means working outside the traditional denominational and institutional structures. She doesn't want to be a deaconess in a cathedral doing Christian education. That gives you a second circle —outside traditions.

From there you add two more circles. She wants to work in an urban environment, and she wants very much to be part of a community team that is experimenting with re-creating a sort of Acts chapter 2 fellowship.

Now that her circle of vocation diagram has been drawn, you can point her to sources of information about inner-city Christian communities, street work, relief agencies, hostels for battered women and evangelistic missions to transients and ex-prisoners.[2]

Aptitude Plus Training Equals Occupation

It will rarely be sufficient just to draw circles of vocational interest to determine careers, however. You will have a fuller understanding and appreciation of career choices if you examine also your aptitudes. It is important to understand who you are and what you're

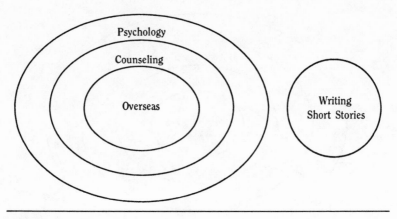

Figure 6.

good at. Probably you'll need to increase your competence by getting training appropriate for the career you are choosing. In a sense, we have a theorem here: Aptitude + Training = Occupation.

Some sort of formal assistance is probably mandatory if you want to know your aptitudes. Choose one of the standard helps that is available. (The appendix lists published resources for career decisions.) Then, just as you used the circle technique to determine your *interests,* use it to zero in from your peripheral *aptitudes* to your central ones, from nice but not necessarily useful training courses and experiences to those that are kernel to the issues of getting a job in a certain field. Using the circle of vocation approach in conjunction with such a handbook as *Life Planning* is an excellent way to tackle the problem of choosing a career. That smorgasbord may not be so bewildering as we thought!

Open Circles
Early in the fall term the UBC students explored circles of vocation. Sheila, majoring in psychology, was able to draw three; but then she had an unconnected circle of ambition, which we decided to draw alongside the major focus. (See figure 6.)

Steve was already fairly certain of his circles: "My circle of voca-

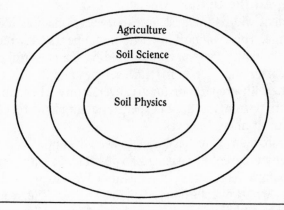

Figure 7.

tion is agriculture. I'm in soil science; my area of interest is soil physics, and my bachelor's thesis is on the water balance of Peace River pasture." So we drew this (figure 7).

Rob was hesitant. "If such a circle existed, it would probably be teaching. Probably not religious studies, though. But something related to the arts—at university or college. I just want to keep as many avenues open as possible." All we drew was this (figure 8).

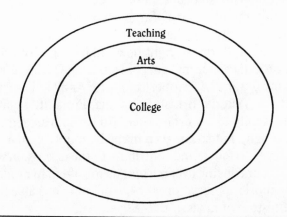

Figure 8.

Keeping All the Options Open

The student who is the best prepared vocationally is like a Swiss Army knife. Those ubiquitous little implements with red handles bearing the white cross of Switzerland have a powerful mystique. From Switzerland—land of Heidi, watches and Zurich gnomes— they come with a reputation for great versatility. They can do everything from opening bottles of expensive champagne to, yes, taking stones out of horses' hooves.

Like Rob, many of us have tried to keep the options open, to take in as many different experiences as possible, to gather under our belt as many different courses as possible. We have wanted to be like the Swiss Army knife: flexible, adaptable and versatile, ready to turn our hand to anything, ready to pull out of our wallet some sort of skill or qualification that will fit us for whatever career we eventually pursue.

It is a formidable challenge to take this approach, for it means hard work and constant effort. It means being alert and open to everything, always ready to absorb, to try and to learn. Biting off as much as possible can be scary. But read this letter from a friend studying at the University of Ottawa. See what it looks like to be such a student, getting ready to tackle the world of work with a full complement of skills and education.

I'm heading into my fourth year at the U. of Ottawa in history. I've got a scary workload ahead of me but September is always the calm before the storm, so right now I'm feeling very optimistic and enthusiastic about my year. I'm studying Quebec literature, Quebec history and Latin American history—all in French. After 4 months in Victoria, British Columbia, I'm a little concerned about my ability to "se débrouiller" [to get into something and see it through], but so far, even in my honours seminar course, I've managed to follow and contribute to the discussion without getting lost or tripping over my tongue too often. In English, I'm studying music appreciation, the history of Canadian education and the history of modern China.

Outside of school, I've taken on a part-time job as a second-language monitor, helping Francophone students learn to speak, read and write English. I've been placed in a high school not far from here where I work primarily with foreign students from Haiti, Zaire and France. Most have been here only a few months and speak very little English, but they are keen to learn. And I am keen to teach.

Teaching is one route I'm seriously considering for next year or the year after. I'm still eager to try my hand at journalism, though, and I've been collecting experience in that field by writing for our school paper and working for the summer in the communications division of the B.C. Ministry of Energy, Mines and Resources. Then there's the possibility of law, foreign service, and, oh, the list is endless. The only thing I know for sure is that I want some time off school to travel and seriously think about all these choices.

Analyzing the Scare

Several things strike me about that letter and the girl who wrote it. First of all, I grant you that Lauri is a gifted and capable student, and she might have more options than the average C+ student. (Being capable is, in its own way, a little scary.) Yet she is just as obviously no slouch! It is to her credit that her energy, drive and discipline allow her to choose the number and variety of courses that she has, and that at the same time she engages in worthwhile (but demanding) extracurricular activities. Although all these activities are in and of themselves valuable, let's see how it all adds up vocationally.

Lauri is studying in two languages at a bilingual university in a country that is officially bilingual, Canada. This opens up the whole area of working in the federal government, in any of the provinces (including Quebec), or in international affairs that might involve French-speaking nations. But it has cost her energy and commitment to accomplish this, because she comes from an Anglophone part of Canada (Victoria, B.C.), and she had to cross the nation on a three-thousand-mile journey into newness to enroll at the University of Ottawa.

Next, because she knows that teaching is a possibility, she is volunteering in a high school, using her language skills, gaining educational and international experience, and providing herself with a future entry on her résumé that will look good. Simultaneously, she gets to find out whether teaching per se is the kind of thing that she will really like. She realizes that journalism still attracts her, so she keeps that option alive by writing for the school paper. At the same time she has some background ambition about law and public service, and her course choices are building an appropriate context for such a future.

Last, Lauri is decisive about one thing—the need for time off, to travel and think seriously about her future. From what we garner about her from this letter, we don't expect her to be wasting her time in complete idleness in Greece or Italy or France. Underlying her whole approach to her education (and presumably her approach to life) is an attitude of daring and determination, daring to take the risks and choose the harder route, determination to squeeze the very last drop out of her university training and student years.

"Keep the options open." "Go for the gusto." These clichés seem appropriate for Lauri. And looking at her from an employer's point of view, we see a girl who could more than likely succeed at a whole variety of careers, a girl of quality and adaptability, of endurance and stamina, a girl who is educated in the best sense of the word and for whom there remains only the matter of choosing before she enters the final training that will take her somewhere near the top of whatever career she reaches out for. In other words, we see a prospective employee who is just the person we need. So we choose her.

Specialization: Now or Later?

The student who is best prepared vocationally is like a dagger, a single blade of steel with a single purpose. No use looking for corkscrew or screwdriver functions when a dagger is what you want. It's as single-minded as an ICBM.

This argument diametrically opposes the idea that the best-prepared student is like the multipurpose Swiss Army knife. I write the contradiction deliberately to highlight the debate that exists regarding the best way to prepare a student for his or her career. The conflict is this: are we best prepared for getting a job by being well rounded through a generalized education, or do we need increasingly to specialize at earlier and earlier stages in order to present ourselves for entry into a career with enough intensive, specialized training to allow ourselves a chance of succeeding? It is the breadth-versus-depth argument.

I have always favored the generalized approach to education, believing that the essence of education lies in that well-rounded familiarity with the major ideas in science and the arts which was the hallmark of the Renaissance man.

Many years ago I was helping a farmer on his farm in northern England. As we prepared to spread manure by shovel over the grassland, the old farmer said, "You can either cover all the grass with a little muck, or you can cover a little bit of grass with all the muck. But if you dump it all in one place, you'll just burn the soil and leave the rest of the field starving." My idea of a good education is one that "covers all the grass with a little muck."

Theoretically, a well-rounded education, a true university experience, ought to prepare a person for any career. Like a skier at the top of a mountain, able to ski down any of a dozen possible trails, a graduate should be able to head off into many possible careers. An editorial in *Christianity Today* supports the liberal arts concept of college education. Specific skills, says Kenneth Kantzer, are temporary vocational tools which increasingly become outdated. "The person who is best equipped to function effectively in the marketplace of the future will be the generalist who has not only learned his economic skills, but who is also equipped by his general education to be flexible enough to make moves from one vocational skill to another as the economic picture changes."[3] A broad education is an education for life.

However, contend the other voices, it appears more and more that such a broad and diverse education as I have suggested can leave a graduate unprepared for the specific requirements of any one career. And so we have all those Ph.D.'s in history and art appreciation driving buses and selling cosmetics. Can you really get a job with a general B.A. anymore? The tension between the views is real.

Obviously, it is far too late to leave all preparation for career until the day of graduation. A current television advertisement shows a young man receiving his degree at a college convocation. Dreamily, he remains seated as all leave. Then his thoughts—as if for the first time—turn to the skies, to flying, and we see him presumably choosing to join the U.S. Air Force (who sponsors the ad).

It is too late to be dreaming vocational dreams on graduation day! The time to begin thinking seriously about career is at the beginning of your university education, not at the end. You need from the start to choose courses with both goals in mind. First, select courses of value, courses that will challenge you, educate you, round off your knowledge in a whole variety of areas, give you the option to choose all sorts of directions later in life. Second, at the same time, measure the vocational importance of your education and select courses that will build a cluster of qualifications that begin to head off in a particular, specialized direction.

Varying careers make different demands with respect to the breadth or depth of your preparation and training. Those which require graduate training and have a premium on well-rounded, intelligent preparation (for example, law, medicine, administration, public service, industrial and business management, personnel work, pastoral ministry, teaching, social services) are best prepared for initially with the sort of approach that Lauri took. Other fields, probably those of a more technical nature (aerospace technology, advanced physical and chemical engineering, microelectronics and the whole silicone chip revolution), will demand more specialization at an early age.

Good, hard information will help. As you enter your first year at college and begin to think seriously about preparing for a career, shop around and "get the facts." Find out what sort of training and preparation is best suited for the careers that you might be interested in pursuing later. Become informed now and plan accordingly.

The Jobs for the 1990s

What jobs will be open to career seekers in the next decade? Probably not those that were expanding fields in the last decade, as we saw in chapter two. Nor is it likely that they will be spin-offs of those humanities courses that have enriched your university career. So while you delight in being on campus amid intellectual and artistic stimulation, keep in mind these five suggestions from a recent article in *L'Actualité*.[4]

1. Get as much education as possible. Realize that most professions are training and retraining their workers continually. (Hydro Quebec sends its technicians back to school every two or three years to keep abreast of technological advances.)

2. Get math, more math and even more math. It is "the royal road to all the careers of the future."

3. If you choose to specialize early, don't specialize in a dying profession, one that will not exist in the nineties, and don't ignore the rest of your education while concentrating on a specialty. You need to be educationally flexible to survive progress. Four of the five jobs available in the nineties have not yet been invented! And no longer will a worker do the same thing all his life. You will need to change and adapt, and you can do this best if you have a solid educational base.

4. Become the best. Excel! It will be a heavily competitive job market in the nineties, and the best jobs will go to the best people. Choose a quality education, collect good courses and do well in them. Study hard and accomplish.

5. Be prepared to move. It is highly unlikely that you will work out your career in your home town, or even in any one town. You must be prepared to relocate.

The study goes on to list the nine career zones that are increasing in our decade and which offer great potential for recruits in the 1990s: (1) engineering; (2) microelectronics and information processing; (3) biotechnology; (4) physics; (5) agricultural technology and food production; (6) aerospace, telecommunications and marine engineering; (7) health; (8) environmental concerns; and (9) business and commerce. These careers are on the increase, evidence of the effect of technology and science on today's professional patterns.

On the wane are the humanistic fields. Law, social science, teaching and anything in the arts-recreation-literature-journalism quartet are all diminishing in terms of the number of new jobs for new entrants. The part of the job market that is diminishing fastest is the civil service. Because of the changes in political philosophy and the general public abhorrence of growth in the public sector, abetted by the sort of tax revolutions that are typified by Proposition 13 in California, public service will be a diminishing source of employment over the next decade or two.

There is room, however, for optimism. There will be jobs in the 1990s, hundreds of thousands of them, available for any man or woman who puts his or her mind to getting educated, getting trained and getting a position. While no one can deny the importance of technology and science in the career world of the closing twentieth century, let me repeat my plea regarding that well-rounded education: Let us have biotechnicians who hum Bach, mathematicians who muse over Marianne Moore, programmers who peruse Pascal. And *I* will promise to learn how to use a word processor!

4

What Is This Thing Called Work?

Mennonites are in favor among Christian employers in Canada. Why? Because Mennonite young people have the right attitude toward work. They work hard and they work well. They are used to taking responsibility; they know how to roll up their sleeves and get their hands dirty. And they stick with a job until it is finished.

When I was directing the Inter-Varsity Boys' Camp at Pioneer Pacific in British Columbia, we really appreciated having Mennonite students work in our kitchens and on our staff crews because they did not continually have to be told to get to work. They cooked the first pancake and wiped off the last counter. They made the run up to the tanks for gas and cleaned up the wharf at the end of the day. They were good.

"Thank God I'm a Country Boy"
At a recent lunch with an engineer I came to realize that John Denver's song "Thank God I'm a Country Boy" had vocational import. With my engineering friend, who was soon to be made vice president of a pipeline company, I talked of recruiting good engineers.

"How come you did so well?" I asked.

"I was lucky. I was a farm boy who got a good degree."

"What does being a farm boy have to do with it?" I asked, surprised.

"Farm boys are the best in our business. Any engineer who is looking for a job has an advantage if he comes from the farm. Give me sixty engineers looking for a position in this pipeline business, and I immediately ask for the ones who come from farms because they're the ones who have had to work ever since they were kids. They've been given chores, responsibilities. They've had to do a man's work without anyone to hang over them and nurse them along. When I was fourteen, my dad gave me responsibility for the threshing crew—three or four guys working under my direction. Farm boys know how to handle responsibility. They've always been around machines; they know how to fix things and make motors go. And they know how to work. So a farm boy gets a head start when he's looking for an engineering job."

Even allowing for the partisanship, the message is clear. If a person knows how to work hard and well and how to shoulder responsibility, he's got a better chance to get a job.

Don't give up, however, if you are not from the farm. There are other ways to build work experience into your background and to prove that you are a responsible, able and credible worker. Summers offer a good opportunity to establish a respected work record; so does the exercise of a consistent part-time job. As with the formation of all Christian character, each little bit of work you do goes toward establishing a total pattern of habit and attitude . . . and reputation. Build up a reputation for being a good worker. It's important.

Work: a four-letter word, one which most of us instinctively shy away from. Last night, a friend asked me if I was still writing this book. "Well," I replied, "I'm finding it hard to get down to it. The initial stages are over. I've had all the inspiration and the fun of the first burst of ideas and data. Now it's at the hard-work stage, and I hate having to sit down and flog my way through a constant drudgery of writing, rewriting and rewriting again."

That's it, isn't it? We are allergic to work, happily concurring with the old cliché "Ah, I love work; I could watch it all day long." We wonder if work is really necessary in this enlightened age. We wonder if there are ways to avoid it permanently. "It seems to me that a great nonsense is talked about the dignity of work," says a character in one of W. Somerset Maugham's novels. "Work is a drug that dull people take to avoid the pangs of unmitigated boredom."[1] When all is said and done, what really is work? Where did it come from? Is it all as horrible as we think?

I will tell you my opinion. I believe that work is more than necessary; it is positively good. In fact, it is vital, a gift from God without which we are less than whole.

Activity, Work and Work-work

With the students from UBC I had a great discussion about the nature and the theology of work. Let's start with Clark as he gives us his philosophy of work.

"Man is meant to work, as opposed to winning lotteries, or just being rich without having to work. Work is important; it's a means of making a living, of supporting yourself and your family. I should be able to find some real meaning within the work itself, rather than just seeing it as something I ought to be doing, something just as a means to an end. I feel that work should provide a feeling of reward, a feeling that I am contributing to some goal, not only for myself but for the job—that it's helping other people as well. Work provides an opportunity for growth. You're being exposed to people and you can influence people."

Carol: "Work is meant to make you independent to a certain extent, so that you're not a parasite on society. I think my whole philosophy has been entrenched in me from my family: that *what* you do doesn't matter—it's basically how you do it; that you work hard at whatever you do. Beyond that I think it's important to be enthusiastic about whatever you do, to apply yourself to the best of your ability."

Sheila: "I agree with Carol. But in my mind I see a sort of idealized symbolized work, you know, that's just for you. A job where you will find some kind of fulfillment, where it won't be 'life after hours' but life within work that matters. I think we can put up with 'work-work' as long as it's temporary, like a summer job."

Steve: "Work should be enjoyable. It should be an enjoyable part of your life and not, as you said, Sheila, just 'work-work.' It should be a real place where you can be expressed, where your gifts and talents can be used."

Glenda: "I see work as something that eventually should benefit society as a whole. I don't think that I could be engaged in a type of work that did not benefit society. I see the need for a job for myself that will be personally satisfying, stimulating, and that would enable me to grow as a person."

Rob: "I agree with Clark's point that work is something necessary, that has to be done, because I think that we've all experienced at various times God's calling. He calls people to work. And I think that because he's called us to do it, we should do it well. Give it our utmost."

Me: "Now are you two guys talking religiously? Are you saying that God created people to work?"

Clark: "Yes, that's what I'm saying."

Rob: "I think I take exception to the idea that man was created to work, because he wasn't. Work is a result of the Fall."

Me: "Let's just zero in on this because this is one of the disagreements that I meet in my reading. What is your doctrine of work, Rob?"

Rob: "I said that mankind is supposed to work, that we're meant to work. But that was not the plan from creation, not the original situation."

Me: "So work was instituted as a result of the Fall, as a punishment, in other words."

Clark: "I would disagree with you. I think God gave man a task to do, even as simple a task as naming the animals—which you may not consider as work. And what about the tending of the garden?"

Rob: "I don't consider that work. But God says that you shall work by the sweat of your brow, and in that passage it is almost a curse. It is seen as something negative."

Glenda: "But naming the animals was a *type* of work, a *way* of working. Man has to work by the sweat of his brow, but he was working before, just not by the sweat of his brow. It is as if work and play were at first intertwined, and there was no distinction between the two. Now there *is* a distinction, and work has become the more difficult."

Sheila: "And that distinction is because of the Fall."

Rob: "I agree. I would say that the elements of that fallenness pervade our work, and that is why it's so frustrating at times. That is why there's 'work-work' in the summer. We can't get back to that original state. However, I think that in heaven we'll have activities to do but they won't be seen as work. They'll be seen as activities which will result in giving God glory."

Me: "So you don't call the pre-Fall activity 'work'? Are we then just arguing about semantics?"

Rob: "Yes, I don't call that work."

Me: "What would you call it?"

Rob: "Activity."

So there it is! Adam was engaged in activity before the Fall and work afterward—which deteriorated into work-work after the first hour or two of digging in the hot earth. But the shades of difference that are part of the semantic coloring reflect our experience of and attitude toward work rather than work itself. Sweeping out the barn can be a joyous labor of love (yes, even one that brings glory to God because we do it for him and in him!), or it can be the weariest of toil, drudgery, sheer work-work. It may simply be our attitude which dictates.

Work—A Blessing or a Curse?

Many Bible readers see the Genesis account of creation as the theological source book for why we dislike work. In Genesis 3:17-19, work seems to be part of Adam's punishment, a result of disobeying God. Many, therefore, view work as punishment, part of the evil consequences of the Fall. Thus we gain our bread by the sweat of our brow, and work is seen as a curse, an enemy to be avoided, a permanent companion of misery.

I find it impossible, however, to read the Genesis account with this as the only interpretation of the place of work in our society. For surely there existed work in the Garden of Eden before the Fall: how otherwise could Adam have been a steward over the natural creation? Behind the mandate of Genesis 1:28 lies the fact of work; behind Creation itself lies the fact of work.

Would there have been no necessity to sow, cultivate and reap without the Fall? Would the ideal garden not need attending? Would the ideal fruit not need cultivating, gathering and picking? Of course it would. For instead of making a magic place of ease where divinely ripened peaches fell off divinely pruned branches and floated into hands held out in nonchalant ennui, God put man and woman into a living relationship with living things—beasts, crops, insects and fruit. And a living relationship can only be sustained through activity and work, on both sides—by the busy bee and the busy human.

Indeed, the fact of work, and the rhythm of work and rest, are established for us by God the Creator. He is God the Worker. He uses energy as he works to create the universe. Therefore work is *good* because it derives from God. Work has its very source in him. Consequently, we created beings, made in the Creator's image, are to be workers too. "We are God's workmanship, created in Christ Jesus to do good works, which God prepared in advance for us to do" (Eph 2:10). And he who was and is supremely the image of God in the flesh knew what it was to feel the drive of work. "My father is always at his work to this very day, and I, too, am working" (Jn 5:17).

I presume, though, that the pre-Fall lifestyle with its components of work and activity would have been one of harmony, delight and satisfaction, the pleasure of work done for its own sake and for the glory of God. What the curse brought to work was its overwhelming hardness, its toil and drudgery, its uselessness and pain; and what it brought to relationships within work was its vindictiveness and oppression. The curse brought overseers and taskmasters,

masters and slaves. With that change in the essential nature of work came a corresponding change in the human attitude toward work. We came to despise it, loathe it, shirk it. And nature, designed to produce in abundance, ease and fertility, now produces with reluctance, severity and barrenness.

I contend that work is an essential part of the purpose and design of humanity, that we have been made to work, and that work is an essential good. I believe that to be without work is to be bereft in some fashion. That is why I think there is a fundamentally moral evil in any society that can tolerate high levels of unemployment, such as currently plague the Western world. Christians, in particular, have a duty to uphold the dignity of work and to emphasize the constructive role that work plays in our society.

Work can be therapeutic, part of the process by which disturbed or maladjusted people can be taught to develop a fullness and harmony of personality that brings fulfillment. I have seen this idea worked out in a community outreach center that our church operates in Montreal. Just this week Bill, who has spent twenty of his thirty-eight years under psychiatric care, worked in the center for two four-hour stretches making chicken soup. His soup was a culinary success, and Bill glowed with pride and pleasure, knee-deep in compliments. That eight hours of productive work was a miracle for Bill. He had previously managed only two days of work in the last twelve years!

Gene Thomas is a Christian businessman and Bible teacher in Boulder, Colorado, who has developed a couple of small businesses which, in his words, are "designed to lose money." Gene uses them to provide occupational experience for such diverse people as drug addicts, ex-prisoners and the mentally deficient. The person who comes to Gene and his team for work may at first be barely able to stay in one place for ten minutes at a time, barely able to do a physical task for half an hour a week, barely able to communicate with others, barely able to receive instructions, barely able to operate within the context of normality. But slowly, with infinite love and patience from those in charge, such people are made whole. After six months of unproductive, awkward effort, the client reaches the point where he or she begins to work productively, to make a genuine contribution to the small business which has painstakingly hired and trained him. Of course, in the midst of the inevitable chaos that such a business operation maintains, profit cannot be achieved. That is why Gene has other businesses which do produce a profit, for money must be found to support the weaker brothers and sisters while God is putting them together again. But from Gene I have learned, and with Gene I believe, that work can play a crucial part in healing the wounds and hurts of life and in bringing wholeness.

There are enormous political and educational implications if we believe that work plays a vital role in human life. If work is genuinely important to the sense of worth that an individual experiences, then we must commit ourselves to political action, economic development and educational philosophy that guarantee the existence of worthwhile jobs. If a child needs to learn the essential goodness and necessity of work, of contributing valuably to her family, school or community by her own effort, should we adults continue to shield her from anything that looks like hard work or toil? Is not the farm-boy model of useful and responsible contribution one that we should adopt and expand, not only because in its own right it is intrinsically good but also because it is a fine preparation for entry into the adult world of work?

I recognize that finding sufficient meaningful, preferably physical, work for a city child in a housing complex is not as easy as it might sound. Test yourself: how much actual productive work did you do as a child or teen-ager? How much as a university student? Sure, we all took out the garbage and washed the car (as long as dear old dad paid us for it), but how many of us learned responsibility in leading others, caring for living and growing things, fixing things that had to work, building things that had to stay built?

I am grateful for my Merchant Navy training on oil tankers. As a boy of fifteen I left home, and by the middle of my sixteenth year I was left alone in charge of a midnight loading. The oil would be pumping aboard at several thousand tons per hour, under extreme pressure. It was my responsibility to check the levels in the tanks, and to open and close the correct valves in the correct order to avoid a colossal spillage or structural damage. I remember sweating with more than the tropical night air as I planned and replanned the strategy, checked and rechecked the levels. I knew from other people's stories what disasters could happen. We apprentices had our own collection of stories about such things. In fact, I once was involved in the cleanup after a Third Officer made a loading mistake. Yet, because of such experiences, I learned how to work—to work alone, to work responsibly, to work accurately.

Work: Dangerous, Boring, Bitter

If the Fall is viewed theologically as the entry of Satan into our world as author of sin and evil, it is logical to expect that consequent evil has entered the realm of work. So it has. Work can be dangerous.

Some kinds of danger may randomly affect any of us at any time —in driving, in disease, in plane crashes. Random danger may strike at work, too. And certain jobs are unavoidably risk prone, such as those requiring work at dangerous heights or deep beneath the earth or sea. But where workplaces are dangerous for *no necessary reason,* the evil is to be fought, not accepted. Those who work and name the God of compassion as their own should aim to eliminate sources of danger wherever possible. Where safety is compromised for the sake of greater profit, where ignorance or irresponsibility endanger lives, there Christians are called to build safer conditions.

But what of the *deliberate* physical and personal danger of some professions—of police work, for example. It is salutary to read Acts and recall the attendant danger of choosing apostleship as a profession in the first century. (We should speak of "being called into the vocation of an apostle" rather than of "choosing" it.) Read 2 Corinthians 1:8-11 for a summary of the scars that the apostle Paul earned at his occupation. And the history of the church bears glorious record of men and women who have faced incredible dangers to obey the call of God to bring the gospel into certain areas of our world.

We can do nothing but admire those who choose dangerous careers so that they can obey the calling of their God to minister the gospel, or so that they can enforce justice, keep the peace, maintain order, deal with violent and insane persons, or bring the healing of medicine into situations which threaten disease and death for the healer. Such is the sway of evil today that judges and magistrates, lawyers and police officers, and even occasionally a teacher or doctor, can find themselves threatened physically by someone against whom they have declared justice. Are Christians to shun these jobs because of the danger that they presume?

Christians are not motivated by fear of people, but they are susceptible to it. They have to steel themselves to stand on the truth that God's principles of justice supersede the fear of consequences. Therefore, they must account guilty and sentence the terrorist murderer, even though a threat of personal reprisal is phoned to the judge during the case; the junior engineer must report the unsound and dangerous structure that threatens workers' lives even though a superior threatens reprisal; just workers must counteract the control exercised by corrupt union bosses even if violence is threatened to family members. Given the nature of the call to battle on behalf of good against the forces of evil, God's call on some Christians to work in the realm of justice and order is particularly appropriate. May God ever protect those who so do.

Boring! Boring!

Danger, however, is not the threat that looms over most of us as we prepare for our careers. Monotony is the more threatening specter. How can we sit in this same office, work in this same factory, perform this same mechanical function, deal with these same people, every working day for the rest of our lives?

Just this week, in attempting to find a job in a plastics factory for a Sri Lankan political refugee, I was told by the placement officer, "Be sure to tell him that this job is deadly boring. He must know that there's absolutely nothing to it except the same routine all day long. But he must stick at it for at least a year if he wants to get a different job with us."

For a while it was the trend in our society to greet everything that was slightly slow, dull or at an interest level one degree below a Kiss concert with hoots, jeers and cries of "Boring! Boring!" Our young people are terrified of being bored. They have become satiated through their overindulgence in a world of wall-to-wall stimulation. But the UBC students that I talked to were also fearful of landing a job that would be boring. The phantom of the automated worker on the automated assembly line—eyes staring vacantly, mind in limbo, dignity destroyed by numbing purposelessness, hearing ruined by incessant noise—haunts most of us.

"What do you think about boredom at work?" I asked the students. "Is it a sort of *sine qua non?* Is it a built-in essential that you simply have to live with? Are you terrified of being bored in your work?"

Glenda replied first. "Right now, I can't see myself being bored. I just finished a practicum in which there was so much to do all the time, I didn't have time to be bored. I can see myself being totally frustrated and fed up at times—but not bored. I can't see myself ever getting bored."

Sheila was more pessimistic. "I can see myself getting very bored," she admitted. "And it scares me."

Rob introduced a new idea, "I think boredom comes in from simply having a job that doesn't tax you to the limit of your ability. Last year I was doing a job that was creative for a while, but after a time it became somewhat of a drudge, and I had to take an evening course just to keep my mind alive."

"Now," I demanded, "are there any jobs that will not be boring after a while? Let me give you an example. When I was a kid, my brother-in-law was always a bit of a hero to me because he flew fighter planes in the navy. He was in the British Fleet Air Arm, and he landed planes on aircraft carriers. I thought it was probably the most exciting job in the world. But I remember him saying to me, 'No, Mike, it's quite boring. You get in the plane and you take off and you land . . . you take off and you land. Time and time again, the same thing. Quite boring, really.' I couldn't believe it! I still don't, in a way. So, is there any job of itself good enough to keep its interest? Or are we all going to end up like Rob, taking an evening course just to keep our minds alive?"

"Well, there's always bullfighting," Steve offered.

"I think that a job would have to be changing all the time," began Carol, "though I don't know in what way. Like, interacting with the world in a really dynamic way in order to keep from getting in a rut."

"That's probably why we look for a job with some sort of career pattern to it, with promotion and advancement in it," I concluded. "We realize that after four or five years in the same position, we'd like to move into new challenges."

Bitterness

A job becomes bitter when the relationships within which we work are so sour that bickering, manipulation, disrespect, contempt, abuse and dishonesty are the hallmark. A job is bitter when we find ourselves used or exploited, when the human relationships have gone foul. A job is bitter when the very thought of it produces bile and sourness in the stomach. Often our physical sicknesses mirror the psychological realities of our workplace.

A prominent feature in the fallenness of our whole world is that bitterness in relationships. The world of work, where forced relationships must be maintained daily, can carry that bitterness to extraordinary depths. Who will spend a complete life of work without ever coming under the authority of a supervisor who is brutally unfair? Who will never be betrayed at work, unfairly treated, hurt or despised?

Danger; boredom; bitterness. These elements invade our work because they invade our world. We who follow Christ can claim no exemption from the world's fallenness. Christian cashiers get shot in violent bank raids, Christian clerks get caught in mindless monotony, and Christian architects are misused and cheated by their employers who despise them.

The world's full load of unhappiness will spill over onto our shoulders occasionally; indeed, each must carry a share. And there is an inextricable mix between that random suffering that comes our way just because we are human beings and that particular "suffering for righteousness' sake" that is the peculiar consequence of following Jesus. Yet there is meaning in a Christian's difficulties, because suffering produces perseverance, character and hope, making us eligible to share in the glory of Christ (Rom 5:3-4; 8:17).

Our jobs have not yet been redeemed. But we have. Hearing the call of the King, we set hearts and hands to labor in his name, so that the product of our labor and the quality of our relationships may bear the King's stamp.

5

There Are Christian Workers but Are There Christian Jobs?

Really? You don't sound like a Christian!"

When I first received that response to my laid-back, cool, radically different verbal witness, I was impressed and flattered. I thought I had broken through the dead clichés into a realm of poetic freshness, a new gospel.

But when my friend's initial sentence of wonder was followed by his "Actually, you don't act like a Christian either!" I realized that there was room for anxiety. I knew that Christians were supposed to be somehow visible, that they were to be known "by their fruits," that they were to be recognizable as followers of Jesus by their deeds, character, attitude and words. I decided that from then on I'd better be more laid-forward, hot, more in tune and in keeping with orthodoxy. If my life was fruitless, my verbal witness was pointless.

Not only in our verbal witness but also in our jobs, in the way we fulfill our obligations at work, we Christians must be a living, authentic testimony to the Lord we profess. That much is sure. But how does being a Christian show at work?

Christians at Work

For the New Testament apostles working daily at their ministry of evangelism, being a Christian showed up . . . in their scars and bruises. They bore the mark of injury and insult. Their being Christian showed—if not at work, then certainly after it!

Imagine Paul or Silas coming home for supper at the end of Acts 16:16-40. "Had a good day at the office, dear?"

"Yeah, sure. Got seized by two angry businessmen, attacked by a mob, dragged into the marketplace, stripped, beaten, flogged by the police, and thrown into jail. And that was all before coffee break. Here, want to see the bruises? Apart from that, and a miraculous jail break, it was a pretty routine day."

Now we do not bear similar marks of persecution on our bodies as a result of letting our Christianity show, not even those of us who are in "professional evangelistic ministries." And I pray we never shall. But what *are* the marks that you and I, followers of the Lord Jesus Christ, carry with us into our work and maintain as visible distinctives during our employment?

I wrote in chapter four of the general favor in which Mennonite students are held by employers. We certainly enjoyed them as staff at our Pioneer Camps. Their aptitude for work, their positive attitude, their commitment to finishing the job: all this showed as clearly as if they had hung a sign around their necks. Is it true, then, of Christians in general that they should show distinctive characteristics in the way they work? If so, what should these particular distinctives be?

Good Attitudes

Steve started our discussion on this question, tossing out some general comments having to do with Christian character. "We must work to the glory of God; therefore we should give our employer a generous return. Our work should be a witness. Something I struggle with is how Christians can do this when they're collecting garbage every week. I guess by being at peace with the situation you're in, by not saying, 'I just can't wait till I beat out old Joe above me, the dirty, rotten guy.' And by refusing to backbite, refusing to be molded by the system. There's a great pressure to get out there and sell yourself. I guess we don't stand there as sheep and let everyone pass us by, but by the same token we mustn't allow the pressures of our fellow workers determine how we act on the job."

Glenda saw Christians as shiningly honest and as mediators. "I think in our jobs we should be peacemakers between fellow employees—try to be mediators. And we should be very honest in our jobs, honest in returning to our employer the amount of work we do." That, I thought as I listened, is the second time the question of integrity in work effort and work amount has been raised.

Clark argued that Christians brought a distinct set of values with them. "I was thinking that the Christian should at no time let the job become more important than the people he's working with. The people that we're with are far more important than maybe the goal we've got."

Sheila saw and stated the connection between a Christian's integrity at work and her integrity in life generally. "The marks of a Christian at work," she commented, "should be the same as the marks of a Christian in life."

"Great point!" I exclaimed. "Now, what are the marks of a Christian in life?"

"I don't even know if I know," she continued hesitantly. "I think of genuineness, and honesty, and love, and patience, and virtue—all these kinds of things."

Rob was more precise: "I think of the difference in terms of goal orientation. The goal of a Christian is to glorify God, not just to put meat on the table or to fill up time or to make life less boring. Ideally, Christian workers should not be alienated, in the Marxist sense of the word. They're not put off by work because they know who they're working for."

They know who they're working for. Some time ago a representative of the Canadian Automobile Association came into our church outreach center (a rented storefront) to try to sell subscriptions to his association. He met Richard, a Church Army (branch of the Anglican church) student from Toronto, who was directing the project during the summer months. Richard explained that he didn't even own a car and therefore couldn't really respond.

"What about your boss?" queried the salesman, pushing a little.

Without a moment's hesitation Richard replied, "God? He doesn't need a car!"

They know who they're working for. That is crucial for Christians. It means that we regard all work, no matter how menial or socially demeaning by some standards, as being our vocation. We are called to work. Therefore we work for him who does the calling, the Owner of the vineyard. Others—like Alcan, IBM, Canadian Pacific, U.S. Steel—are really underemployers, the Employer's helpers, if you like.

Our vocational ambition like our life's ambition, is to glorify God. At work, as everywhere, we want it to be known that we work for and belong to God. And we make that known by the attitude with which we engage ourselves in our work. How depressing and unauthentic it is to have someone working in a Christian setting, where all are ambitious to glorify God (as at a Christian camp, for example), with anything less than complete energy and enthusiasm! It is only our inner attitude which can turn work into work-work, or vice versa. Our outer attitudes, those which are on display, will quickly let our fellow workers know what our values are. Can we glorify God by cheating on our hours' slips, sneering at a junior, casually taking home an item of merchandise here or there, hastily doing a shoddy job because we have to rush off to a church meeting or even a "Happy Hour."

"Whatever you do," writes Paul in Colossians 3:23, "work at it with all your heart, as working for the Lord, not for men." Brother Lawrence, a seventeenth-century Carmelite monk, tells in his *Practice of the Presence of God* how he learned to work for the glory of God in his community's kitchen, elbow-deep in greasy dishes or scrubbing the filthy floors.[1]

Good Workmanship

I would hope that a Christian worker would be visible in more ways than through his attitude. I would expect a Christian worker to display his or her faith and values through the quality of workmanship. This does not mean that a Christian has to be the very best performer, the very best artist, the very best carpenter, cook or caterer. The quest for supremacy is too heavy a load for us to carry, and it is no part of the call of Christ. He does not push us to vocational supremacy. But a Christian's work has to be good, good in the sense of whole, complete, thorough—the best possible.

Can a Christian be a shoddy worker, a poor artisan, an unsatisfactory employee? G. K. Chesterton once joked, "If a thing's worth doing, it's worth doing badly." He meant by that to encourage us to try our hand at an endeavor that is of itself worthy, without waiting for the time when we can do it with guaranteed success. But this witty and ambiguous saying is certainly no glorification of incompetence and was never meant to be a motto for a Christian worker. Rather, we take the original aphorism: "If a thing's worth doing, it's worth doing well."

Do we imagine Jesus the carpenter taking short cuts, making ill-fitting joints to save time, pretending to customers that ash is oak, failing to take a full share of clean-up duties at the end of the day? No, of course not. The Christian man or woman must (I say *must* because authenticity demands it) display integrity in workmanship, honesty, thoroughness and fairness. As the worker embodies these discipleship values in faithfulness to Christ, the Master will become visible.

Time and time again, we followers are enjoined to be like the Lord; we servants are to be patterned after the Master (see for example, Mt 10:25). Imagine with what infinite care, thoroughness and craftsmanship God fashioned the universe. Our daily routine of work must somehow be an imitation of his.

Can a Christian Perm Poodles for a Living?

A Christian's faith ought to be visible both in the quality of workmanship and in the attitude demonstrated toward work. But we must raise another question: Is a Christian's faith to be made visible in the *type* of job he or she does? Are there such things as *Christian jobs*? Are there careers that a Christian ought to gravitate toward and others that are ruled out-of-bounds?

Many sincere disciples of Christ maintain that some careers are simply too frivolous for Christians. Christians are to be about the serious business of establishing truth and justice, bringing in the ethic of the kingdom, binding up the wounds of the world. Any job which panders to excessive materialism, conceited egoism or listless dilettantism is impossible for a follower of Jesus whose values of sacrifice, service, humility and dignity forbid such pandering.

I agree with this argument. The job of a lifetime, that is, the sum total of the effort produced by our hands and minds over twenty-five to fifty years, is wasted if all we are offering to the world are face-lifts for tired, rich, bored women and fur-lined putting wedges for the Man Who Has Everything (except his soul). Christians especially must pursue for the major part of their lives a work that has inherent value.

Some career choices pose moral dilemmas of varying intensity; here the question of frivolity is replaced by the stark question of ethics. While there is no question that a Christian cannot be a pimp or a strip artist, or a dishonest anything, one Christian's set of values will perhaps collide with another's on the question of working for a winemaker or tobacconist, a lottery board or a theater. Or, pertinent today in view of the Nestlé boycott and Love Canal, can a Christian work for a multinational corporation which oppresses poor workers in a Third World country or for a chemical company which makes napalm or for the military-industrial complex? In today's complicated world of intricate commercial relationships, where business interests are intertwined across the globe, how do we begin to answer these questions?

The Chain of Connection

The first pointer I want to suggest as we struggle with these questions concerns the extent of what I call the chain of connection. Some police officers are brutal and corrupt. Does that mean I can never join the police force for fear of being part of that evil? In

South Africa, the Bank of Montreal is connected with the financing of mining operations in which Black workers are shamefully treated. Does that mean I cannot work as a teller at a branch in Montreal for fear of being party to that exploitation of cheap labor? Worse still, does this distant connection mean that I cooperate in injustice and bear a small part of the guilt if I even put my money on deposit with a local branch of the Bank of Montreal? Will I be under judgment for so doing?

The immense complexity of our world, with its finely tuned network of financial interrelatedness, traps us all in this dilemma. Near where I live, Bombardier makes skidoos, subway cars for the New York Transit System, and armored vehicles for warfare. The shipyard makes tugs and frigates; the high-technology factories make computers for hospitals and missile systems. For most of us, as workers, there is no escape from the dilemma. If we trace the links far enough, we find ourselves connected to evil. There are virtually no virtuous, untainted work worlds where all is, in Matthew Arnold's words, "sweetness and light."[2] To work at all, most of us will become involved with huge, industrial, global conglomerates who have at least one finger in the pies of mischief, oppression or warfare. Is this giant, worldwide vocational complex illicit for a believer? Is there a way out?

Laurence Shames, writing for *Esquire,* concludes that there is not:

Is there a decent way out? Short of retreating to the forest and living on roots and grasses, is there a way to avoid even the occasional brush with devil's work?

I doubt it frankly. Things are too thoroughly intertwined. Let's say a fellow does a perfectly moral job for a company that's owned by a conglomerate with an objectionable component or two; however faintly, he's tinged. Albeit indirectly, I am in the employ of everyone who advertises in *Esquire;* what if I have ethical gripes with some of them? I'm stuck. Each of us is dependent for his or her paycheck on a vast network of forces, not all of which are blameless—and to share in the rewards is to share in the taint.[3]

Biblical theology teaches us that we share a common humanity, one that is universal. We share, too, the undisputed worldwide effect of sin; its taint touches us all. Even for born-again Christians there is no respite, no glass-screened, even-temperature haven of holiness where at least our patio is clean.

Still, as Shames writes, "there are degrees of complicity, and degrees matter." If the chain attaching us to the injustice is short, we have to quit. If it is long and sinuous, I believe we can be judged blameless.

I do not believe that the industrial-commercial complex of global business is, in toto, an illegitimate sphere of work for a Christian. The chain of connection joining the eighteen-year-old bank teller in Montreal to the ugly oppression at the Johannesburg mine is too long and too tenuous to exclude bank telling as a valid career for a child of God. In cases where the chain of connection is inordinately long, I believe the Christian is absolved from complicity.

But the overseer who whips the Black worker in the mine shaft is guilty. For him the chain is so short it has become the direct moral link between the whip in the hand and the stripes on the back. The difficult question is, of course, How short does that chain have to be before I am guilty? Different instances will have different answers. Lurking behind all our thoughts and debates are the pathetic excuses offered by the Nazi war criminals and their minions: "I wasn't really guilty; I was just obeying orders." But the hand that does the violent act is the guilty one, whether obeying another's order or initiating its own. The hand that lashes with the whip is guilty; so, too, is the hand that holds the victim; so, too, is the hand that places the whip in the torturer's hand; so, too, is the hand that prepares and greases the leather of the whip. We must all be careful that our hands have not been guilty of short-chain contact with evil in our workday. In Shames's terms, we must not be guilty of "devil's work." For

Who may go up the mountain of the LORD?
And who may stand in his holy place?
    He who has clean hands and a pure heart,
who has not set his mind on falsehood,

and has not committed perjury.
He shall receive a blessing from the LORD,
and justice from God his saviour. (Ps 24:3-5 NEB)
I believe, then, that the answer to the question about culpability lies in the directness with which we are involved in evil. We are responsible for our own actions. Each must decide for himself or herself when that chain of connection has become so short that a job must be refused or left. That development of individual moral judgment is part of our Christian growth and maturation.

If you have a sincere doubt as to a particular job (and let us all beware our skills at self-justification and rationalization), seek counsel, prayer and wisdom from elders. Ask the Holy Spirit to lead you. If we must err, let our error be made on the side of sensitivity to evil. If in doubt, get another job.

Once persuaded in your own mind that a certain career is frivolous or unethical for you, stick to that decision—no matter how tempting an offer might come across your path from Hooker Chemicals or the Pittsburgh Poodle Emporium. If it is your prior personal conviction that chemical wastes, dangerous radiation risks or poodle puffery is an illegitimate pursuit vis-à-vis Christian stewardship of God's created world, resist the temptation to submerge your ethical sensitivities beneath a fat payroll with a cost-of-living-allowance clause.

In today's recessional economy, the temptation to set aside your principles in an extremely tight job market is fueled by the panic of not being able to pick and choose jobs anymore. The voice of compromise might whisper, "It would be okay to take just a tiny little job making napalm. . . . After all, there's just nothing available anywhere else . . . and it's so unchristian to be unemployed . . . and I'm sure they use napalm agriculturally somewhere . . . " No. It is unchristian to change principles according to panic; it is unchristian to change principles to accommodate circumstances. It is thoroughly Christian, rather, to arrive at our principles of what defines legitimate employment for ourselves, hold them fast and trust God to guide us as he honors our stand for righteousness.

Other Persuasions

Christians will differ in their answers about the ethical virtue of certain jobs. The question of military service is one such divisive issue. The media made much of the fact that the officer who led the British attack on the Falkland Islands carries a New Testament in his pocket at all times and prays daily. At the time of the invasion Roman Catholic priests were giving mass to the defending Argentinean soldiers. "Whose side is God on?" is the classic wartime question. For the Christian, confusion about military service is compounded by the possibility of fighting an enemy who also professes the Christian faith. For this and other reasons some Christians have declared themselves to be uncompromisingly against joining the armed forces or supporting them in any way. Others, however, see the armed forces as a noble career, one which defends the right of the nation to a Christian expression. All I can conclude is that individuals have the right to their own decision, and the empirical and historical evidence suggests that Christians have always differed on the issue, still differ and probably always will. It therefore seems invidious to me for one side to judge the other.

Naturally, if a Christian chooses the military for a career, he or she will have Christian ambitions within that career. His or her ambition will be to glorify God in everything, to soldier with compassion, honesty, fairness and gentle strength. Yet the trap of complicity with evil will be waiting. How can you be honest, compassionate and gently strong when your finger fires a missile which flies a hundred miles to a target you cannot even see? How long are the chains of connection that tie you to a village massacre, an indiscriminate bombing raid? Nevertheless, the Christian soldier must try to absolve himself from personal violence and cruelty, dishonor and avarice; and many men and women of God have in duty, in uniform, shone forth like lights amid the darkness of warfare.

"Let every one be fully convinced in his own mind," writes Paul, in Romans 14:5 (RSV), commenting on disputes that had arisen concerning foods that some Christians were eating and the attitude that some had toward the Lord's Day. This principle of inclusiveness is appropriate when assessing the various attitudes that believers will have toward different jobs. We are not to be each other's judges, says Paul. We all belong to the Lord, and each will live his life to the Lord's glory. There is no one single stamp of unity on the vocational choices of believers. We choose freely. We choose differently.

Choosing a More Challenging Way

Being a Christian at work relates not only to *how* we work and *what* we do. It also relates to *how much* we work and *why*. Up to this point we have looked at a career as a five-days-a-week, eight-hours-a-day proposition. But more and more Christians are seeing this as an outmoded goal. The limited job market and the need for more volunteer Christian workers have convinced people to become more creative in their vocational choices. And many Christians see this as a new opportunity to live a life that is more focused on God's will and less focused on the day-to-day demands or the distorted values of the marketplace.

Far too often our standards and ideals, worth and identity, methodologies and lifestyles, are determined by external influences. A prestigious job makes us feel important. Total job security makes us feel safe. A large salary makes us feel valuable. The correct job title gives us our identity. But security, worth and identity come not from the externals of this world but from the inner reality of what God has done for us in Christ and from what we have appropriated to ourselves by faith. Therefore, we ought to look at the world from the inside out, holding up our faith like a giant magnifying glass, examining, measuring and evaluating all of life through its truth and power.

By turning around our thinking we can begin to conceive of a career as a means rather than an end in itself—the means to support us financially so that we can carry on another ministry. In his challenging book *The Mustard Seed Conspiracy*, Tom Sine describes an assignment he gave to his students at Seattle Pacific University.[1] He challenged them to create a ministry in which they could imaginatively respond to an area of compelling human need. That ministry was to take them thirty hours per week. Then they had to devise a way in which they could work at paid employment for twenty hours each week to support their ministry. Such a challenge is the sort of radical change in thinking that I am suggesting here. Suppose we do deliberately cut back on our paid employment to increase our involvement in church ministry. What if we take a risk with employment? What if we free-lance or create our own small business?

The cost of this more challenging way is obvious. It means a substantial reduction in standard of living. For unless you have an extremely well-paying job, to work only three days a week means earning about sixty per cent of what you could be making otherwise. Can you survive on a sixty-per-cent income? Can you raise a family and enjoy enough material security to avoid sleepless nights on three-fifths of your earning potential?

Choosing Sacrifice

You can live simply. You can undoubtedly live more simply than you are now. You might even be able to cut back to sixty per cent of your income. How? Lots of books will tell you how to start. Chapter one of *Beyond the Rat Race* by Arthur Gish has some helpful suggestions.[2] You can follow the example of people like Walter and Virginia Hearn, whose experiences in deliberately reducing their income are recounted in *Living More Simply*.[3] In 1971 Walter was a tenured professor and research scientist at Iowa State University, embarrassed by his affluence though happy in his work. Convinced

of their personal calling to simplify their lifestyle, within a year
Walter and Virginia had pared their expenses by half. But a simpler
lifestyle was not their primary ambition. Conscious of the temptations of low-income spiritual one-upmanship, they saw clearly that
their faith commitment was to Jesus first and foremost, not to a
simple lifestyle. A call to an unencumbered lifestyle is one way to
live out our love for and obedience to Christ. But it is never an end
in itself.

Walter Hearn gives six reasons for his change of career: (1) he
was convinced God had a special purpose for him and his family;
(2) he grew concerned about the apparent pointlessness of his work;
(3) knowing that "anyone in whom God's spirit is active should expect to change with time," he had the sense that the university
phase of his life was at an end and that the next career step was to
try full-time writing; (4) he had an ever-growing delight in simplicity; (5) he wanted to devote more personal energy to his family; and
(6) he had a sense of adventure and a willingness to try new things.[4]
So he resigned his position and waited for God to speak. The uncertainty of those early days and weeks was sickening. But God did
speak, leading him and his family into a lifestyle of faith that has
become a model for many.

The Hearns later made it into the headlines of the *Los Angeles
Times* under the dubious title: "Ph.D. Scrounges for a Living." Not
everyone understood their choices. But they experienced great joy
in a life which reduced itself to finding practical ways of buying
food and cooking, recycling materials, sharing with others, and
doing without all those unessential but attractive things that assail
our eyes and ears through the media. Virginia Hearn relates one of
their most memorable anecdotes:

> For his fourteenth birthday, our son, Russ, invited a friend out
> for pizza. Then we took the two of them to the edge of the city
> dump. "Since it's your birthday," said the Last of the Big-Time
> Spenders, "you can have anything you can find. Good hunting!"
> Hours later, Russ came back with a phonograph turntable in
> perfect condition. His friend thought it the most fabulous

"birthday party" he had ever been to.[5]

Recently I hired a bookbinder for a government-sponsored project connected with our church outreach center. Janna is a thirty-year-old woman who is easily noticed in our Sunday morning congregation by her unconventional clothes and short, gray hair. She loves all handicrafts and loathes the mechanical sameness of most modern industry. When she started work, she already seemed to have much of the material that she needed. I asked her where she got it. She replied that she scoured commercial garbage dumps and was often able to find great quantities of excellent materials that she could recycle into her work. "Besides," she said, "that fits into my philosophy of voluntary poverty. You just use what others discard."

Choosing a Simple Lifestyle

In April 1979 a hundred evangelicals met in Ventnor, New Jersey, for the U.S. International Consultation on Simple Lifestyle, a conference which had its roots in paragraph nine of the Lausanne Covenant of 1974: "All of us are shocked by the poverty of millions and disturbed by the injustices which cause it. Those of us who live in affluent circumstances accept our duty to develop a simple lifestyle in order to contribute generously to both relief and evangelism."[6] *Living More Simply* is the collection of reports and addresses from that consultation, and it is must reading for any who wish to answer the call to simplicity. It will help you respond to the question, How do I start simplifying my lifestyle?

The best way to get started is to keep an accurate account of all your expenses for a month or two. The major ones are easy to keep track of: rent or mortgage, phone bills and insurance, utilities and gasoline. The tricky ones are the out-of-pocket transactions—that spontaneous stop at the restaurant, that impulsive shopping, that little bit of spoiling. These are the ways a great deal of money can be spent without our realizing just how much.

A friend of mine saved carefully to take his family of four to a theater in the old section of Montreal. They had a wonderful evening and thought they would cap it off with a stop at a posh hotel for coffee and dessert. Before they knew what had happened, they had spent over half the cost of the four tickets on just a little ordinary coffee and everyday cheesecake. Driving home they vowed to take their own snacks next time. So be careful to list, and then control, the little items.

As we said earlier, however, simplifying our lives is not an end in itself. It is instead a means to the end of better serving God. Changing your expectations of material comfort and altering your career goals will be big steps. But they will also challenge your faith and cause that faith to grow. Faith cannot be grown in total security. There simply will be no occasion to use it. Faith can only be tested (and through testing comes growth) amid genuine need, helplessness and the adventure of launching out. Read the old saints and talk to the saints around you. They know. If you want to launch big boats, go where the water is deep. Faith calls you to deep water. It calls you to a creative, wholly God-centered approach to careers.

Choosing Creativity

A group of Christian doctors in a rich suburb decided to do their work "Christianly." They now share earnings, each taking somewhat less than he could, so that every year one of the group may go to serve in a mission hospital in a Third World country.

An elementary school teacher reduced her teaching load to part-time so she could help organize and run a Christian bookstore in her small town.

An Inter-Varsity staff worker with a heart for ministry in China dedicated himself to becoming a specialist in teaching English as a second language to Chinese speakers. He has just returned from Peking, having taught and shared the faith as much as possible. "As a Christian, I saw my time in the People's Republic as a venture of service in the name of Christ," he reports.[7]

A businessman in Colorado runs a deliberately smaller operation than he might so that he can be free to be a Bible teacher and conference speaker.

All these examples illustrate creativity in approaching work and career. They illustrate the radical reversal of putting career and job second to a call to ministry. Radical thinking demands creativity. So does following Jesus. "Every Christian has a ministry calling," writes Tom Sine.[8] That means some will be challenged to change jobs, others to cut back working hours and reduce spending. It means challenging accepted views of career. But above everything else, it should mean that every area of the life of a believer centers around a ministry to God's kingdom. The objective is simple: to make enough money to be able to spend a greater amount of time and energy in serving the Lord and being part of what he is doing in the world. The way to accomplish that objective is less simple. It is here your ingenuity must come to play.

You really have several options. First, you could develop a commercial enterprise you can own and operate with strict controls (so that it doesn't get too big and imprison you in its demands) and with efficient production (so that it makes a profit and provides an income). Dozens of examples come to mind. A Christian student put herself through college by getting a contract to paint and repaint all the fire hydrants in her home town. A cooperative group at a church developed a print shop and book bindery. From an Anglican church near Montreal, a group has emerged to act as consultants to churches who are venturing into computers to do word processing and accounting. Young people from Victoria, British Columbia, established The Sonshine Kids to do painting, commercial clean-up and house repairs while providing income as they grew and worked as a Christian community.

Another option is selling your time and energy as a service. That means working for someone else. But you can work less than full-time or you can take extended holidays without pay so you can serve at summer camps or short-term mission projects. You might become part of a work-sharing scheme, where two people fill one full-time position.

A third way is to sell the product of your hands. A friend of mine is a carpenter and joiner, but such a good one that he is able to live quite happily by taking only a few special contracts for handmade furniture. That frees him to give time directly to God's service. Another friend paints portraits—good ones, which sell well—and this allows him ample time to be active in his church. Dancers, musicians and other creative people of all kinds can look for outlets for their skills which will provide them with salaries (though the competitiveness of these fields will definitely test their faith). And these artistic folk can contribute to the mission of the church. There is unlimited scope for accomplished artists, musicians and actors in liturgy and evangelism.

This radical approach to careers has its own cutting edge, though, for it brings with it the insecurity of being without a regular or full-time salary. But it is the Lord's glorious right, responsibility and privilege to care for you, honoring you in your need as you honor him in his service. And where does all this lead? To freedom.

Choosing Freedom

So much of the gospel message speaks of freedom. The fundamental freedom is freedom from the wages of sin. But the freedom that seems hardest to enjoy, perhaps because it seems the least attractive, is freedom from materialism—freedom from anxiety about food, shelter, clothing, transportation, housing and financial security. Jesus said, "If the Son sets you free, you will be free indeed" (Jn 8:36). And surely *indeed* means really free, free from all the shackles that bind us, including those of materialism and anxiety.

In *Freedom of Simplicity* Richard Foster praises the untrammeled life.[9] Standing strongly against what he calls our passion to possess, he lays out the biblical groundwork and theology of simplicity, turns his attention to both its inner and outer features, then explores the ideals of a simple church within a simple world. His thesis is as clear in the book as it is in his title. If we can shout "Stop the world, I want to get off," if we can make that giddy leap from speeding madness into steady sanity, we will find an indescribably wonderful freedom.

The madness of the world is to make a career out of "acquire," to spend all —money, energy and, yes, even love—on the getting of things. The cool sanity of Christ is to make giving our goal, for it is in giving self over to him that we truly find, are found, and receive all that we have ever yearned for.

Getting There from Here: Guidance

Some of you will begin this chapter (I say *begin* because half a page should set you straight!) with enthusiasm, with anticipation, with the expectation that a foolproof, theologically sound system of guidance will be unraveled before your very eyes. This chapter will be the one you are most anxious to read, the one that you will read most avidly because you are longing to learn how to be really guided by God. Some of you are reading this page almost in despair, for you are face to face with a situation demanding a most difficult choice. You feel so lost, so vocationally uncertain, that you come to these pages with anxiety, a fretful longing for that special answer to be revealed right here, on these pages, and . . . Yes! . . . you should take that part-time job as a Santa's Elf at Sears, for there you will meet a theatrical magnate (masquerading temporarily as Santa) and your longed-for career as an actor will be miraculously launched. You will be discovered overnight. A success! A star! And all because of this chapter and that part-time job at Sears.

Forget it. I'm sorry; I should not be so peremptory and abrupt, if not downright rude. What I mean to say is that I am embarrassed about this chapter because of its possible ineffectiveness in solving your guidance problem. I'm afraid I do not know any foolproof systems of guidance. And I have probably made more tortured, mistaken lunges at "being led" than the average person following a half-trained seeing-eye dog. Certainly I've had pieces of guidance in my past; all sorts of strange things have led me along my path. But system? I cannot see one. All I can see is a potpourri, a kaleidoscope, a higgledy-piggledly collection of principles, exceptions, attitudes, actions, Scriptures, prayers and final decisions that, put together, make up the sum total of God's guidance in my experience.

I know, too, what it is to be almost in despair about a decision, groping wildly for a sign, a message from Divinity. At times my spiritual senses of guidance have been so acutely tuned that every tiny stimulus has been taken in by my receptors as significant. Did *National Geographic* feature Iran this month? That's where to go. Did the TV (casually turned on) show a National Film Board vignette about Manitoba? I should take that job in Winnipeg. Did someone like my joke this morning and tell me I ought to work with kids all the time? It's guidance!

Well, it might be. But there is no guarantee. There are no systems. And sometimes our intensity to be guided is our worst enemy. In that enormous drive to find significant guidance in "signs," our minds can interpret data in such an irrational fashion that we respond to trivia in unchristian ways.

A Relaxed Confidence in a Heavenly Father

Our Christian strength throughout all of life, but especially in matters of vocational guidance, is our attitude toward security. Our attitude corresponds to a fact: the fact that God is there, permanently and unfailingly, caring for us. "The LORD is good," writes Nahum, "a refuge in times of trouble. He cares for those who trust in him" (Nahum 1:7). Zephaniah and Zechariah confirm that "the LORD Almighty will care for his flock" and "restore their fortunes" (Zech 10:3 and Zeph 2:7). Peter urges us to cast all our anxiety on God, "because he cares for you" (1 Pet 5:7).

Our response to the fact of God is relaxed confidence. We sink into those everlasting arms like a pole climber into his safety harness, an old man into his comfortable armchair, or a child into the arms of his father. "The eternal God is your refuge, and underneath are the everlasting arms" (Deut 33:27). Our eyes run along those everlasting arms to the hands that hold us, and we see on the palms of God our very own names (Is 49:16). He cares for us by name!

Every minute of every day the Father is guiding us, and the fact of guidance is just as important as its technique. The fact is that God is there leading us not only in those anxious days of scary decision, not just in the cross-country moves, fantastic promotions and incredible first opportunities, but in all things. And "all things" includes the humdrum necessities and boredom of our daily toil. Therefore, as you read these pages, you can willfully and confidently relax into the hands of God, for right now, even this very moment, God *is* guiding you. His hands have no breaking point, as ordinary hands do. He can cope. All the events, feelings and thoughts, all the drama of your week, are in his knowledge, and it is the Father's responsibility, one might almost say his duty, to guide you. As an intimate counselor he will take you through the small moments of each day, but also as one who has all worlds and all times in his control.

It is probable, however, that he will only slowly reveal the size and scope of his purpose for you. For the secret of all worlds and all times is his alone.

The Lost Asses Adventure *(fifth in importance)*
Many years ago a farmer's son called Saul went looking for some lost asses—and found a kingdom. Some piece of guidance that was! You can read about it in 1 Samuel 9. Paraphrased, the story runs something like this.

Saul's father had told Saul to go and look for the lost asses, probably because a few lost asses represented quite a hole in the old farmer's balance sheet, and capital losses couldn't be written off as a tax break in those days. So Saul took off, calling "Donkey, donkey, donkey!" as he went. He and his servant jogged a fair distance donkey-less, seeing nothing. Nothing that looked like a donkey, that is. They jogged so far that Saul suggested they turn back.

"Let's go," he said, "or my father will stop worrying about the asses and start worrying about us." Nice son, Saul.

The servant said, "Nope, not yet." (He was a pretty emancipated servant.) "Let's go and check out the local seer."

Now a seer is supposedly a religious nut, a supertuned guy who gets messages about lost asses, kings, and stuff like that. So, checking in the pocket of his robe to verify that he had enough loot to tip the seer, Saul agreed to go and talk to him.

While all this was happening stage left, there are some goings-on that Saul knows nothing about. God has been talking to Samuel, the seer, who isn't a religious nut at all. In fact, he's a pretty O.K. prophet. God's message is a little cryptic. He says to Samuel, "At this time tomorrow, I will send you a man from the land of Benjamin. Anoint him prince over my people Israel."

Oh, oh! You know what's coming now, don't you? It's like watching a corny old western unfold. Yep. When Saul arrives at Chez Samuel, he's told, "Forget the lost asses; they've already been found. Have a kingdom instead." Now Saul hadn't even opened his mouth to mention any lost asses, so he thought it was all pretty spooky. Anyway, it proved that this guy was a good seer (that is, he could see properly; he could *fore*see), and it saved Saul's having to fork out the tip that he'd got in his pocket. Then, in the morning, Samuel anointed Saul king over Israel and sent him off with directions about a lunch appointment.

I find this a fantastic event in terms of guidance, especially from Saul's point of view. What possible idea could he have had that this particular journey was going to end with a crown? None at all. First Samuel 9:21 records Saul's amazement. God is always at work leading his people, all his people, not just special ones like kings, in his own unique manner. And the principle of guidance at work here is surely this: What might appear to one individual to be a completely fortuitous or chance event is seen by another as part of a specific purpose, initiated and directed by the Almighty.

What does this mean for you and me as we take the bus downtown to the library or drop in at the employment office? It means that vocational guidance can come to us out of nowhere. It means that the loving Father, in whose care we relax, is capable of leading us to exactly the right place at exactly the right time for some momentous reason. What, you might ask, if Saul had found the asses before he got to Samuel? Or if they'd never escaped in the first place? Or if the father had sent a different son? Then we presume that God would have chosen another method. No trouble, really, for a God who is actively involved in the affairs of his world, for a God who is imaginatively creative and authoritative.

This lost-asses principle of guidance, then, is a biblical way in which God can provide vocational guidance. But it is a "spectacular aberration from normal experience," in Philip Yancey's words, "hardly the type of incident to construct a philosophy of guidance around."[1] This leads us into our next useful principle.

The Happenstance Principle *(fourth in importance)*
Happenstance is a novel Old-English word, a combination of "happen" and "circumstance"; it means "chance." There are "chance" events and coincidences in the lives of Christians that take on a significance out of all proportion to their apparent purposelessness. Perhaps this is another way of making Shakespeare's point: "There is a tide in the affairs of men, which, taken at the flood, leads on to fortune."[2] But Shakespeare had more intentionality to his tide and to its taking. I am talking in this section of events which guide a Christian and yet which seem to be sheer contingency.

Let me give you two examples of this principle. On a Tuesday in February of last year, I was planning to run a Boys' Camp Weekend reunion which was to take place the following Friday. Unfortunately, we had only six boys registered at the time, so we decided to reduce the weekend by one day, taking the boys out on the Friday and Saturday only. Then Bruce, one of the leaders, asked me if I would like the weekend off. Such a small number of boys did not require large numbers of leaders. He had other leaders and offered to direct the weekend himself. I thought the offer was great, and I eagerly accepted, anticipating being able to spend the time at home with my family.

On Friday morning, three or four hours before I would have had to leave for the reunion if I had been going, a friend phoned in despair. He was in the middle of an acute emotional breakdown and felt suicidal. Because of the "good fortune" of being released of my responsibilities about the camp, I was free to drive over to his apartment. I brought him back to my house for the weekend and cared for him, helping him to bridge this particular crisis and developing a means of helping him over the next few weeks.

Without that "lucky break" of Bruce's offer to lead the weekend himself, I would have been away all that time. Would he have phoned someone else? Would he have conquered this crisis in another fashion? Would he have attempted to take his life? Who knows. But in a series of apparently chance events God was obviously guiding things and people to fulfill his purposes.

A similar event of contingency became meaningful in Clark's life over the Christmas holiday. Let him relate the story.

I filled in an application form with the Workman's Compensation Board. I'm really interested in what they've got to offer. I heard about this job in an interesting way. I was hitchhiking, and the fellow who picked me up was one of the people who do the hiring there—which was very nice. He was explaining some of the opportunities to me (this was before Christmas), and he invited me to call him up.

So in January I called him up. He explained the jobs more thoroughly and took me on a tour of the place. Then he explained the jobs I might be interested in. He said that if a job came up, I should apply for it, and he'd try to push for me to see that I at least get an interview. So I've got kind of an "in" with him.

Here again we meet that principle of happenstance. A Christian student, with no thought of seeking vocational guidance, just happens to hitch a ride with a man who does the hiring for the Workman's Compensation Board; and suddenly Clark, with his psychology degree and his career interests, fits right in. Opportunity knocks.

It is our eyes of faith and our understanding of how God works purpose into all things which change the vocabulary from "luck" to "guidance." We could insist on being cynics, even Christian cynics, and claim that these occurrences are simply contingencies, random fortunes. Or we can light up the scene with the eyes of faith and declare that, because a loving Father is constantly guiding the affairs of his children, that which might seem to be chance is, from a theological point of view, an act of guidance. This, I think, is the more Christian response. All of which adds some security to the delicious adventure of life, doesn't it?

The Direct-Message Principle *(third in importance)*
The growth of the modern communications industry has given us a model of message sending and receiving that we would dearly love to copy for those moments which require vocational decisiveness. Just as it is possible in our technological world to beam messages off satellites and employ computer relays to tell anyone anywhere exactly what we want him to do, so we long in the spiritual world to receive communications from God that are as direct and precise. We want, in fact, a teletype printout of daily divine directions. I remember so often saying to God (the direct message is easier from us to him), "Look, I have no intention of disobeying you. In fact, I am eager to be absolutely obedient to your will in this matter. But for heaven's sake (or actually, for mine), please just tell me what you want me to do. Directly."

The Bible is—or can be—the worst book on these occasions, for it is filled with that deceptively simple and mischievous intro- duction "God said." Then follows a direct message. Read the Moses saga for examples: or look at Acts 8:26. An angel, in the Acts inci- dent, simply interrupts Philip in whatever he was doing and says, "Start out and go south up the road that leads from Jerusalem to Gaza." Now, aren't you envious of that sort of thing? Have you ever heard an angel say, "Take highway 401 west, exit 69 north, and apply for that job at International Truckers"?

What does it mean, exactly, when it says "An angel said . . ."?

Did Philip think this message in his head with so much certainty that he ascribed it to an angel? Did he visibly see an angel, so that if he had had a video camera the whole thing could have been recorded . . . in color and stereo? Or is this a poetic, typically first-century religious way of describing a decision that was made purely at the level of Philip's own rationality? And where do those questions leave us? If Philip was able to receive a direct communication from God, can we?

I am sure we can. God is a communicative Being. He speaks, "uttering words that express His will in order to cause it to be done."[3] One of the things that we learn from the Greek idea of the Logos (a title used by John of Jesus in the prologue to John's gospel) is that God speaks through the living Word, Jesus. The author of Hebrews writes, "In these last days he has spoken to us by his Son" (1:2). Jesus used the ordinary elements of human language to communicate truth. Now, in the postascension era, truth is communicated through the Holy Spirit. He is our resident, live-in guide, counselor and instructor (see Jn 14:17, 26; 15:26; 16:13). It is certainly part of our Christian conviction that God is able to speak directly to us.

The varieties of ways in which we get this direct message are many. For some it will be the inner, mental assurance that follows a request for the Word of God to speak; others will really hear words, see visions or have the awareness of a heavenly visitor. A common way of hearing God directly is to have words of Scripture suddenly "light up" with an astonishing immediacy. The words of a Christian friend, of a book or record, can work similarly. In all instances, though, the word will come with its own sense of power and authority; it will be God's word, and you will know that.

Many cautions are probably needed. One is this: you should expect God to lead you regarding your vocation in ways similar to those by which he has led you in all other things to date. Don't run off and change your denomination, throw yourself into the Catholic charismatic movement or a Brethren assembly in a desperate attempt to get tuned in quicker and louder. Do not chase after other people's styles. Stay in the mode that you are used to. If you have never received a vision or heard a voice, it is doubtful that you will now, even if you are in panic about choosing Chattanooga or Chicago. At the same time, there might well be a connection between the gravity or criticalness of a decision and the directness with which God speaks. (But I warn you again, there is no system.)

We can, however, increase our skills in discerning the voice of God; we can develop that aspect of our Christian life which reinforces the communicative nature of our faith relationship with God in Christ. We can practice (or learn) the meditative mode, the quiet waiting on God, the searching of Scriptures to hear the word of the moment, the fellowship of prayer, the addition of extra depth to our Quiet Time. Let me recommend *Celebration of Discipline* by Richard J. Foster as an excellent manual about spiritual growth.[4] The anxiety that typically comes with vocational decision making can become a wonderful training ground for developing intimacy between ourselves and our Lord.

A cursory reading of the Scriptures will quickly show us that the records of salvation are filled with people who have directly heard the voice of God. But there are obvious reasons why God refuses to lay out our complete futures before our very eyes . . . or ears. "It would be cheating at the most basic level of human independence to receive 'the inside story' of how the future will turn out. There would be no meaningful opportunity for faith or obedience if I knew the inevitable result of taking one sort of action and not another."[5]

History is filled with the relics of charlatans and deceivers who claimed to know the future. While those who claim to hear God should never be ridiculed or scorned (they do stand on biblical ground), neither should all they say be accepted with credulity. God's direct revelations always have a moral tone; they declare his righteous will. As such, they are visibly moral. Therefore, messages claimed as God's words must measure up to his standards. The counterbalance of Scripture and church provide healthy safeguards against excessive autonomy or individualism, providing yet another way to check out those who claim "God said" for doubtful actions.

Coming to a Mind on Things *(second in importance)*

Followers of Jesus are social beings. By God's act we have been joined together with other people and called—not just called, *made into*—the body of Christ. We belong to each other, and any Christian who insists on remaining isolated or separated is necessarily suspect. We live and worship in Christian groups, and groups can be sources of excellent guidance about vocations.

Once again Acts provides a model for us. It is not surprising that Acts is a good source book for problems of guidance because there were some serious vocational decisions facing the Christians of the first century. With the radical break from secular society that conversion brought, with the complications of their expecting Jesus to return any moment, everything about the early Christians' economics, jobs and future was up for grabs.

The opening chapters of Acts picture a group of Christians living in harmony and unity. Although this perfection might be rare in the history of the church (which has become almost a byword for disunity), we ought not be cynical about recreating that ideal. God calls his people to be one. Our task is to strive for that goal. This ideal unity is expressed, for instance, in Acts 4:32: "The whole body of believers was united in heart and soul" (NEB). Their unity is expressed again in Acts 5:13: "They used to meet by common consent in Solomon's Portico [porch]" (NEB). "By common consent": that is our ambition. Decision making which comes out of this type of oneness (the consensus model, if you like) carries its own authority. We can act on it with certainty.

This idea of common consent is practiced by a church famous for its renewal. At St. Paul's Church in Darien, Connecticut, the new rector, Terry Fullum, was determined that no decision would ever be made about life and worship unless the church leaders were unanimous. This was a tall order, as the old guard was opposed to "this newfangled idea of being led by the Spirit." But Terry persisted. Anything less than unity over a decision was taken as a sign that further prayer and thoughtfulness was needed.[6]

You can find great confidence in taking a decision that comes with agreement from "the brothers and sisters." Do not hesitate to take your problems to your church fellowship so that others can pray with you and "come to a mind" on your decision. "It seemed good to the Holy Spirit and to *us*, " say the apostles and elders in Acts 15:28, which is a fine explanation of any decision involving a Christian. All this I take to be particularly appropriate when you are struggling to make a vocational decision that has a strong component of Christian ministry attached to it—choosing a seminary, thinking of a mission agency, contemplating offering yourself for ordination.

If you feel free enough to bring a vocational problem to a group of your Christian brothers and sisters, I believe you will be greatly strengthened and will hear the voice of God as he speaks to you through his Son's body, the church.

But I must sound a caution. The purpose of sharing problems with your Christian brothers and sisters is to hear God's voice through them, not just to hear their voices. I do not want to give an impression that you should hand over to others the responsibility of making your own vocational decisions. Your membership in the body of Christ, the "bearing of each other's loads" style of living, does not mean that you abdicate the rights and privileges and responsibilities of being a free, moral agent.

There is currently in the church some teaching about shepherding that can take one to the extreme position where all decisions —about career, marriage partner, children—are handed down by a group of elders. This is an unhealthy and essentially unbiblical understanding of church authority. It substitutes the authority of the elders for the authority of God, and it takes away your freedom in Christ as if it were a bad tooth to be abstracted. Jerram Barrs writes this warning: "Giving church leaders an authority which is more extensive than God's Word commands will cause problems. . . . Instead of becoming dependent upon the Holy Spirit, [people] will become dependent on human leadership." Barrs's book *Shepherds and Sheep* gives an excellent, balanced approach to sharing decision making with Christian friends.[7]

Wise and Willing *(first in importance!)*
Christian guidance is not all mysticism and meditation, contingency and consensus. It takes healthy doses of plain common sense.

A biblically educated reason is your primary tool in making decisions vocationally and otherwise. People make decisions through the use of reason, plain thinking. Therefore, to think Christianly, and to make Christian decisions, we need to educate our reason with the principles of truth that the Bible holds, and then we must add as much sensible information as is available.

In making a vocational decision, first assess the situation as thoroughly as you can, making sure that you understand completely what is at stake. Second, think long and think deeply; assess the probable ramifications of each possibility. A biblically educated reason can prevent your landing unprepared and unqualified on a near or distant shore just because you were emotionally moved by a gospel film.

Although I have given biblical examples of happenstance and direct revelation, the major way in which all Christians are guided is through their "sanctified reason—that is, reason dedicated to serving God."[8] The search for guidance is not a quest for "magic, short cuts and genie bottles" (to quote Philip Yancey's article again), but an exploration of possibilities with our Christian minds operating out of a committed relationship between ourselves and our God. We have a God-given mind, even, as Paul dared to say, "the mind of the Lord" (1 Cor 2:16). Use it well.

Finally, no search for guidance will be successful unless it is accompanied by a real willingness to be obedient to God's will once it is known. To approach God for guidance with a hidden agenda or a flat refusal to take option B is to cast yourself in the role of rebel, hypocrite and liar. It is notoriously difficult to hear the Director's voice in such roles. You cannot expect God to write your script if you persist in perfidy.

The quest for guidance presupposes a genuine willingness to obey the voice of the Guide. We must have already answered yes to God's questioning of our obedience before we dare ask our own question, What is your will, O Lord?

I've Got the "I Don't Know Where I'm Going but I'm Going Nowhere in a Hurry" Blues

Steve Goodman's funny song tells the story of a woman graduate in physics who traipses from one job interview to another only to be continually told, "You'd make a great secretary, Honey."

Many of us know what it is to be belittled, ignored, slighted, ridiculed, disparaged or even insulted in our search for employment. We have cheerfully and earnestly offered our best, only to be rejected amid the mocking laughter of victors. In the middle of a job search life may seem particularly unguided. At those times it is hard to have that relaxed confidence in a heavenly Father.

So what can you actually do when guidance seems hard to come by? Let's try a step-by-step approach.

1. Affirm to yourself that God does care for you and is actively guiding you. First-century Christians were called the "people of the way." The way that we travel is not created totally by ourselves, as if life were merely the sum total of our choices and decisions. We are actually put into God's way: partly by our own decisiveness to stay in the way (Is 30:21; Mic 4:2); but mainly because God is deliberately shaping our lives according to his purpose (Ex 23:20; Ps 32:8). You are right now (unless consciously disobedient) in his holy way.

2. Try to live each day as a conscious follower of the way. Be intentional about following Jesus. Build solidity into your devotional and ethical life. Before you read today's employment ads, visit Manpower or rush off to your thirty-third interview, take time to be in God's presence, in the way. And do some good as you go.

3. Try to bring together all aspects of guidance that you know. If necessary, write down the instances of happenstance, the direct messages, the mind of others, the results of your educated reason. Synthesize the information if you can, avoiding undue concentration on any one special hunch or fuzzy feeling. Round out the picture.

4. Check your willingness and your desires. Do you really want to be guided, to be obedient? This is a toughie, and it calls for rugged honesty.

5. Relax. God *is* guiding you. Go back to step 1.

When Guidance Goes Sour

Decision making produces its own kind of anxiety and nervousness. Much of that anxiety surrounds the unspoken fear, What happens if I make the wrong choice? What shall I do if what I thought was guidance in January turns out not to be so in March? Do I get a second chance? Can I choose again?

The Vocational Prodigal Son

A certain man had two sons. And the younger of them said unto his father, "Father, give me the price of an airfare to Tangiers, for verily I have heard tale of a Process Control Systems Analyst's job, to work closely with creative leaders in the field of microcomputer systems (both hard and soft) with a state-of-the-art company, and reporting directly to the vice president. I feel verily called by God. And I can do evangelism with indigenous tribes on the beach. Besides, much filthy lucre appertaineth thereto, with considerable foreign service allowance." And his father divided unto him the cost of the airfare.

Not many days after, the younger son gathereth all together, packeth his Adidas bag, sayeth farewell to the folks at the office where he worketh, and tooketh off for a far country. For the first while, he wasteth his substance in furious outpourings of energy at work, in finding an apartment, in filling in forms for medical insurance, and in occasional riotous living. And when he had been there a half year, there grew in his soul a mighty famine. Much discomfort about his vocation filled his heart: he was truly discouraged, disturbed and disillusioned. He was feddeth up unto his ears. He felt that God had not really called him to Tangiers, in spite of the great salaries and overseas allowances that appertained thereto.

And when he cameth to himself, he said, "How many guys in the office back home are enjoying their work, and feeling good about what they are doing, and finding a ministry through their employment, and playing golf together on Saturdays . . . and I perish with the curse of a bad decision.

"I will arise and go to my father and say, 'Father, I have sinned before heaven and against thee. Well, not really sinned—I simply made a bad decision and misheard what I thought was the voice of God calling me to a far country.' And I will say that I am no longer fit to be a Process Control Systems Analyst in training, but will humbly take any job as long as I can get back into the old familiar office, and find meaning and purpose in my job, and play golf on Saturday mornings." So he packeth his Nike bag (an indigenous tribe had stolen his Adidas), and he fleweth home.

And while he was yet a long way off, his father saw him, and ran back to the office and slammeth shut the door and yelleth, "Don't let that spoilt kid back in here!"

No, that is not how the original in Luke 15 ends. I just rewrote the ending to shock you. What this unexpected ending can do, though, is reverberate on the strings of our fear about making a wrong decision. We are taught, quite rightly, accountability for our decisions, that every act carries its own inevitable consequences. We are taught to make serious decisions, weighing the long-term ramifications, ready to face and accept all the consequences ahead. But what if you just cannot stomach the consequences, and quit? And what if your father does indeed slam the door in your face? Then you have no job in Tangiers and none at home either. Worse still, you have no home!

In the original parable, the father does welcome and receive his son; the son does get his job back, so to speak. When we move from my distorted literary copy (in which I have pretended a vocational theme) to the theology of Luke 15 and its wonderful spiritual realities of repentance and reconciliation, the message is clearly this: you can always go back home to the Father.

First Choice—First Mistake

The problems of making a wrong choice are particularly acute at the time of leaving university and taking a first job. We get so tense as to whether this decision is the right one. We're anxious about the long-term implications of our first choice, about successful starts or failed attempts, about the usefulness of this first job experience in the light of a lifelong career. We are fearful of making a mistake. Now while I recognize the universality of the "angst" regarding career choices, I would like to take the pressure off you if I can. I want you to take comfort from two principles.

First, all Christians make mistakes, especially in the moral realm. No, that's not pious rhetoric about buying the wrong pair of shoes or forgetting Aunt Ella's birthday. Christians make real mistakes, horrendous mistakes. The Bible is realistic about the ways in which godly men and women "blow it." Both Abraham and Isaac, on their vocational wanderings, got so scared about their personal safety that they lied about their wives and delivered them into other men's hands. King David, prototype of Messiah, sinned all over the place (but especially on rooftops) and degraded the highest office with his lust. Not only do biblical characters sin, making errors in the moral realm, but they also make vocational mistakes.

Jonah, for example, resolutely refused to recognize his vocational counselor and headed off in exactly the opposite direction. Peter denied having anything to do with his Boss, lying to a servant girl through clenched teeth. Then, in his career as a missionary, he was shortsighted about the scope of the gospel and he quarreled with Paul, who saw clearly that Peter was in the wrong (Acts 10:28; Gal

2:11). However, it was to this very same Peter that Jesus said, "You are Peter, and on this rock I will build my church, and the gates of Hades will not overcome it. I will give you the keys of the kingdom of heaven; whatever you bind on earth will be bound in heaven, and whatever you loose on earth will be loosed in heaven" (Mt 16:18-19). I realize that this verse troubles biblical scholars and dogmaticians. There is an historical cleavage between the Roman Catholic understanding of these verses, which emphasizes that the church will be founded on Peter, the saint, the first bishop of Rome, and the Protestant interpretation which broadens Jesus' words to understand the foundation of the church as Peter's confession that Jesus is the Christ. Whichever way you interpret the text, however, Peter comes out of it very well. Yet the same man, just a few verses later, comes in for one of the few personal rebukes that Jesus ever gives a disciple.

Being a believer does not guarantee that we will always make a perfect choice; we cannot do that in the moral realm (that is what sin is: making a bad choice morally), and we cannot do it in the vocational realm. Our very humanness suggests that poor choices will be a constant part of our make-up, even as we commit ourselves to the growing lordship of Christ and the fullness of his Spirit within us. But mistakes do not separate us from the love of God in Christ Jesus our Lord (Rom 8:38-39). Neither will we ever be free from the necessity of decision making. The onus of choice will always be on us. God has placed a premium on the maintenance of our freedom to choose, a premium so great, in fact, that it sent his son to Calvary.

I know what I'm talking about in this chapter from sad experience. I have had two great vocational prodigal-son adventures in my life. Both involved running off to a far country, literally. Both involved leaving a deeply satisfying career only to end up in a horrible position. Each time, I took comfort from fellow Christians who admitted that they too made mistakes now and then. And each time I was deeply disturbed by the believers who callously judged me as irresponsible, disobedient, and thereby proving what they had suspected all along . . . that I wasn't really a Christian.

Second-Chance Comfort

The second principle that you can take comfort from is this: you don't have to live forever in an irrevocable vocational mistake. You can decide to leave and go home. The mistake, in fact, is not irrevocable. You can "call it back." One single bad error does not destine you to the pig trough forever.

Many of us have made vocational choices that caused us unease, misery or guilt. It is a common experience to have taken a job which seemed to promise satisfaction and advancement but actually turned out to be an awful dead end. Perhaps the work was demeaning, mind numbing, physically exhausting or meaningless. Perhaps the boss was a petty tyrant, coworkers were scathingly critical, or the tone at work was bitter or vicious. For a variety of reasons, the promising jobs that we accept—or the obviously unpromising ones that we take out of sheer necessity—can prove to be a terrible cause of heartache and despair. We feel as though we're in that vocational far country.

Sometimes a poor vocational choice has been responsible for our leaving the Father's house in a spiritual sense. It is possible to choose a job that, for one reason or another, leads us away from God, away from our relationship of grace with the Son, away from the empowering and comfort of the Spirit, and away from the mutual encouragement of the body of Christ. Because we are working with particularly attractive and worldly people who are deadening our spiritual senses with their pursuit of the secular, or perhaps because we are being lured into the thrill of making more and more money, or because the prerequisites for promotion demand that we hide our faith, our journey has proved to be a hike into the far country. And the famine of our souls threatens to destroy us.

The gospel, let me remind you, is good news. And the good news is that the Father is always waiting for us to return home. In fact, so great is his longing to welcome us back that, in imagination, we can see him hitching up his robes and running down the dusty road to greet us. No questions are asked (Hey, how much money have you got left?); no guilt is salaciously probed (Hey, how many women?); no penance demanded (Hey, you're really going to have to work 'round here now). Although our pride might be strained intolerably if we return home to the same town, same university, same job, same parental nest, the joy and satisfaction that await us on arrival at our Father's house rapidly eclipse the shame.

You Can Always Go Back, but Sometimes You Shouldn't

For some prodigals, however, the question is whether going home would really be the right thing to do. In other words, have I erred or not? Are these pig-trough difficulties ones that I should escape or ones that I should endure and conquer?

So far I have been encouraging you to understand that a bad or wrong choice of job will not land you irredeemably in a foreign country of misery and purposelessness. You are not condemned to a lousy job for life, as if your career were a prison sentence. Does this mean then that whenever a choice has landed you in a difficult position you should simply give notice and come running home to daddy?

That is definitely not the thrust of the parable in Luke 15. There will be times when the father says to you, quite rightly, "Now, child, you've got to make the best of it. You can't back out and come running home to me just because it's difficult. Tough it out; hang in there. Face life and take it on the chin." (Fond of clichés, this father!)

There's an old, west-of-England joke about a young man who ran away from his farming home to join the army. After a month he had had enough. So he sent this message to his mother. "Sell pig; buy me out." His mother returned the message immediately. "Pig dead," she lied. "Soldier on."

I can still hear my own father's words in a similar situation. I was fifteen and had joined the Merchant Navy and gone away to sea in a blaze of irrational, romantic glory. A year later, having run into loneliness and trouble, I wanted to break my apprenticeship and return home. "Stay," he said. "You'll never become a man by running away." Good advice for a kid wanting desperately to become a man.

What would have happened to the missionary advance of the first-century church if the Christians had retreated to their Galilean fishing villages at the first sign of trouble? What would have happened if those great nineteenth-century founders of missions had stayed at home as professional church-bazaar openers—because it was safe and easy? Would there be a Christian witness on your campus today if earlier students had turned back at the first opposition and huddled in their Sunday-school rooms? Would there be a Christian fellowship at your industrial plant if those who preceded you had become so downhearted at all the swearing that they had packed up their lunch buckets and gone home? It seems to me that the key question to ask when you are considering to act as the prodigal is this: does my job in this far country contain an irrevocable feature that will permanently impair my spiritual relationship with God? If the pig trough is that bad, then it is time to come home. Otherwise, the calling might be to stick it out.

When our family moved from Vancouver—land of beaches, ocean and good old West Coast hedonism—to Montreal (of cold and gray fame), we experienced that far-country syndrome. We felt cut off from friends and our real home. Amid all the difficulties—of trying to master French, of culture shock, of feeling alien, of being marginalized linguistically and politically, of months of unemployment for my wife, of months of going unpaid for me, of government regulations forbidding our children to be educated in English—our spirits sank low.

We had thought that the call to Montreal was part of God's career direction leading to ordination with the Anglican church. The depressing realities seemed to indicate that we were indeed in that far country. We knew that we had not been abandoned by God and that we had not willfully abandoned him, but we felt so lonely and oppressed and unused as witnesses that we saw these as signs that we had deserted the vocational will of the Father. Had we made a mistake? Should we return home to the warm fold of Vancouver and Inter-Varsity? We felt that we should openly admit that we had made a wrong vocational choice and call it a day. (Yes, God was publicly humiliating us in all of this: strong medicine for the soul!)

Then one evening we shared these feelings with a wise and friendly couple as part of our deliberate process of seeking counsel. Judy reminded us that difficult experiences were part of the normal context of everyone's life, especially for new Anglophone arrivals in the province of Quebec, and that they should not necessarily be interpreted as negative signs. In other words, it was not surprising that Elaine couldn't find a job; thousands of other Quebeckers were in the same position. The economy was in a recession, and jobs were simply not to be had. In fact, layoffs and cutbacks were the rule of the day. That Elaine was sharing an experience common to thousands was not to be taken as a sign that she should return to Vancouver. Similarly, that our children were subject to language laws, as were all children, was not a sign that they should be educated in British Columbia. We were feeling lonely and alien? Well, hardly surprising! We had moved three thousand miles away from our rich and satisfying lives out west. Anyone in that situation would feel a sense of loss and would have to grapple with culture shock and the overwhelming newness of everything. We felt our ministry of evangelism to be empty? Of course. Eight months of full-time study at the Diocesan College was bound to take us out of the mainstream of full-time, paid, "professional" ministry. Furthermore, and this was Judy's most telling point, what were we going to make of all the points of guidance that had led us to Montreal in the first place?

We learned something that night: the message to the one who feels like a prodigal is sometimes that he or she is not. We hadn't left the Father's home in any real sense. We had only left Vancouver. This far country of Montreal was the place where God's will—and his grace—were to be found for us as a family. What we had run into was difficulty—plain, old-fashioned trouble. But it was not a sign from God that it was time to go home. Rather it was a testing ground of our loyalty, a preparation for our service, a training for our further ministry. We were, in fact, already home.

Attitude, Not Geography

So there it is. If you are convinced that you really are a vocational prodigal, that a bad career choice is taking you away from the Father, go home. Do not even wait to pass Go and collect your $200; hightail it back to the Father. But if it is just Old Man Trouble you've run into, "hang tough." God's grace is sufficient for you. Though *your* endurance and faithfulness might be under test, his never fails. Read 2 Timothy 2:11-13.

No vocational decision will irretrievably take you away from the Father's care and love. Twice in John 10 (verses 28 and 29) Jesus declares that his sheep can never be snatched out of his hand. Sometimes, nursing the bitterness of a decision which feels bad, we think that God's almighty purpose for us has been eternally thwarted, that we are on a second-rate track for the rest of our lives—perhaps squeezing ourselves, if not out of the Lord's hands, at least to the distant finger tips. But all the stakes do not hinge on one bet! You cannot destroy the sovereign love of God by a single roll of your vocational will. There really is no such thing as a second-rate Christian life because of a single bad vocational decision.

It was John White in *The Fight* who taught me that finding the will and purpose of God is much more a matter of moral attitude than geography.[1] God is much too big to have his will voided because you choose to work in Regina instead of Los Angeles. God will grow you and use you anywhere, for he is the God of everywhere. In the words of a banner that I saw in a church in Montreal, "Bloom where you're planted."

Caught between the Scylla of our intensity to obey God and do the right and the Charybdis of our horror of becoming lost and doing the wrong, sometimes we let fear paralyze us. We allow the specters of poor decisions, bad choices, awful consequences and resulting darkness to overwhelm us. The numbing anxiety of terror binds our feet and ankles, preventing us from ever stepping forward at all. This fear can be especially acute for those who have already made an earlier error, who still walk in the shadow of a failure.

There is a wonderful description of this kind of fear in Susan Cooper's book *Silver on the Tree*. In this children's fantasy which involves a search for the Crystal Sword, whose presence will enable the Old Ones to defeat the Dark, we find the boy Bran listening to Gwion's explanation of how the King of the Lost Land, an unparalleled craftsman, had originally made the sword. But the Dark had entered the king's mind, convincing him that he had erred in making the sword and that he had forfeited forever all creativity and craftsmanship. Gwion continues,

> They showed the maker of the sword his own uncertainty and fear. Fear of having done the wrong thing—fear that having done this one great thing, he would never again be able to accomplish anything of great worth—fear of age, of insufficiency, of unmet promise. And gradually he was put into despair. Fear grew in him, and he escaped from it into lethargy—and so hope died, and a terrible paralysing melancholy took its place. He is held by it now, he is held captive by his own mind. Despair holds him prisoner, despair, the most terrible creation of all.[2]

What can I say to you who live in the paralysis of fear? I can only tell you what the Bible says and then give you a spiritual image. St. John tells us that "perfect love drives out fear" (1 Jn 4:18). Rather than struggling with the meaning of "perfect," or seeing this as yet another of the Bible's impossible demands to absoluteness, concentrate on the idea that all love, perfect or otherwise, springs from a relationship, and that it is out of relationship to God that fears are banished. It is not that we have to surmount our fears by the effort to create our own love, but that he who IS perfect love commands their removal.

The spiritual image, then, is this: we are children, scared of the future, discomforted by the past. We look up into the eyes of our heavenly Father. His eyes are kind, his face is strong yet gentle. He leans toward us, reaching out his arm and hand toward us. "Take my hand," he says. "I am here for you." Perhaps slowly, but with

growing confidence, we reach out our own hand and place it trust-
ingly into his. We hold tight. We are safe, secure. Once again, but
still holding on, we turn our eyes toward the road ahead and take a
halting step forward. We are on the move again. Unparalyzed.

Surprises

One thing that should never surprise us is that there are surprises. Life has taught us to expect the unexpected. One day last fall I attended a conference at a Jewish synagogue. And who should I meet first but a fellow Anglican minister! His response: "Where else would you expect an Anglican clergyman to be on a Monday morning?" I was further surprised by the conference host when he told us not to worry about whether our cars were parked legally, as he had "arranged it with the police." Then the main speaker, a Jewish scholar from New York, proceeded to read from Matthew's Gospel and tell us how Jesus had superseded the righteousness of the Pharisees. All this on a Monday morning!

That same week I visited a retreat house that gives hospitality to alcoholics who are homeless and destitute—and found myself sitting next to a once-brilliant cabinet minister. That same morning as I looked over the shoulder of an old down-and-out man as he huddled for warmth in the Metro, I caught him reading the New Testament. And with me constantly was my own sense of vocational surprise: that at this time, a little past the age of forty, I was being ordained into the Anglican church.

114

Many surprises are less pleasant than these I've mentioned. They can, in fact, be downright depressing: that your boyhood hero has been arrested for rape, that your ideal couple has split up, that your father has been laid off, that the cost of raising a child from birth to eighteen years is $212,328 Canadian![1]

But I believe that deliberately and consciously to set out to know God, to obey his will and to follow his direction is to live regularly with his surprises. It is in God's very nature to surprise us by intervening in our lives and leaving us astonished and delighted at his works. In Isaiah 42 and 43, within the context of prophecy regarding the Suffering Servant who will bring deliverance, the prophet writes these words from God:

> See, the former things have taken place,
>   and new things I declare;
> before they spring into being
>   I announce them to you. (Is 42:9)

> See, I am doing a new thing!
>   Now it springs up; do you not perceive it?
> I am making a way in the desert
>   and streams in the wasteland. (Is 43:19)

And in response to God's newness, his surprises, we create our own songs, like biblical psalms, returning a new song to the Lord.

Saul's Graduation Day

Imagine. A warm spring day in Tarsus, Cilicia. The class of 25 is graduating. (No, that's not 25 people, nor the year 1925; its just A.D. 25.) Among them is Saul. With his bachelor's from U. of T. (that's Tarsus, not Toronto) and graduate studies at U. of J. (you guess that one) under the world-renowned Ph.D. Gamaliel, he is ready to receive his graduating honors in his hometown celebration and move out into the world of work. The future looks promising. His wealthy family has been able to prepare his entry into a career; he is a member of the original fraternity Phi Alpha (Pharisees, that is); he is at home in three cultures and fluent in three languages—Hebrew, Greek and Latin; and he seems destined for a prominent career in rabbinics, religion or law.

So what happens? He becomes a sort of hit man for the Sanhedrin with a contract out on the Christians . . . until the hit man hits the dust of the Damascus road and meets Jesus as his Lord. Surprise, surprise. What happens then to his illustrious career? What vocational trauma lies behind the blinded eyes?

What's in a Word?
God's surprises tend to have a hard edge to them because they are designed to shape us into the image of his Son. He cannot do that by giving us only boxes of candy wrapped in pink bows, or first-class career jobs at the top of the heap.

If we did a word study on *surprise* as it is used as a translation of the Hebrew in the Old Testament, we would find that it means "to be made silent, speechless with wonder, marvel, awe, horror or dismay." These words describe our response to God's acts of judgment in such places as Leviticus 26:32, 1 Kings 9:8, and Jeremiah 49:17 or 50:13. They are associated, too, with the swiftness of his anger, as in Psalm 35:8 or 55:15. The idea conveyed is that of wide-eyed amazement, what the New English Bible calls "being horror struck."

The Old Testament knows another kind of surprise, however, the surprise of delight: like Sarah's emotion at the birth of her child (Gen 21:6), like the Lord's delight in his obedient people (Deut 30:9), like the prophet's breathless contemplation of God's mercy (Mic 7:18-20).

The New Testament brings the quintessential surprise of Immanuel—God made flesh, God with us. Thus the Gospel records are full of people's surprise and amazement at this Man and his acts. Making 120 gallons of wine! Healing on the sabbath! Feeding thousands with a single boy's packed lunch! Raising the dead![2] The etymology of the Greek words used on these occasions (*exhistēmi, ekplēssō, ekstasis*) leads us to see God's surprises as things which "knock us off balance, strike us out of our self-possession, fill us with amazement and wonder, throw our minds out of their normal state into a blend of fear and awe."[3] Hence our English word *ecstasy.*

Knowing God puts us regularly in touch with moments of surprise as we witness the normal made exceptional, the ugly beautified, the demonic defeated, the apparently vanquished made victor. Should we not expect, then, that in our career lives, in our routines of employment and work, similar surprises of God will be found?

Some people are hard to surprise. They are too bitter to be shocked. Eartha Kitt and Peggy Lee made famous a song entitled "Is That All There Is?" The song is a litany of cynicism in which the singer, confronted by the rich experiences of life from fire to circuses, from love to death, sneers, "Is that all there is?" Others, with heart battened down and lip curled up, announce themselves superior and impervious to all possibility of surprise. They are like the Oxford University students in John Galsworthy's novel *In Chancery.*

> We defy you to interest or excite us. We have had every sensation, or if we haven't, we pretend we have. We are so exhausted with living that no hours are too small for us. We will lose our shirts with equanimity. We have flown fast and are past everything. All is cigarette smoke.[4]

Such people hum with the monotony of what psychologists call a "flat affect"; the visual dial of their EEGs shows an emotional flat line. They refuse to be moved or to feel.

Others, however, are alive to all possibilities, all chances of being surprised. Fortunately, Galsworthy describes them also:

> We defy you to bore us. Life isn't half long enough, and we're going to talk faster and more crisply, do more and know more, and dwell less on any subject than you can possibly imagine. We are the best—made of wire and whipcord.[5]

Let us be "wire and whipcord" Christians who wait eagerly for God to leap out from behind the corner of the wall and surprise us.

Reaching Out for Surprise

Surprise means change. To be surprised vocationally means
changes in your career pattern—job changes, changes in location,
unexpected pleasures, unexpected promotions. Sometimes these
changes have their direct source in God's will as he chooses to invade your life with his invitation to newness. Sometimes the initia-
tive will come out of the blue, from an unexpected source. Other
times you will make the first move, reaching out tentatively with a
newborn desire for change, making contact with God and finding
that your desire has his blessing.

Bill Wells did that. In mid life, well into a successful career as a
professor of church history and historical theology at Wheaton College, he was thinking of changing jobs, of moving into the world of
business. It was his eighteen-year-old son's provocative question
that initiated his action.

"Dad," said David, "if you really like business so much, why
don't you quit teaching?"

Doubts surfaced and hovered as Bill moved toward a decision.
Could he pull off this change? Could he leave the security of his
present position? What would friends say at the loss of status and
prestige in the Christian world? Was it really Christian to leave
teaching and enter, of all things, business and financial planning?

Several things were crucial factors in Bill's decision making. He
was not merely fed up with teaching or simply looking for more
money; nor had he lost interest in theology. But he was basically
restless and unfulfilled. The M.B.A. courses he had started taking at
night from the University of Chicago meshed so comfortably with
untapped interests in math and business. Forays into computer
programming were fun. Could it be wrong to follow these God-
given bents merely because they were not on the first path he had
chosen twenty years before?

Bill's family and fellowship group helped him work through the
issues. After much prayer, but willing to take risk in his radical
Christian freedom, he quit his teaching post. He searched two
months before he was offered a position, and then two offers came

within days of each other. He took one offer and became a financial analyst for a downtown Chicago bank.

Was the trauma of the change worth it? Absolutely, says Bill. And while there is still the lingering awe and wonder at such a thorough career change in middle age, Bill knows that he has been led into a career that fits him. Believing that God wastes nothing, he expects someday to see God blend all his gifts, all that he has learned from both careers, into something worthwhile—probably surprising—for himself and the kingdom.[6]

A year after our last taped interview with the UBC students, Clark called me. Surprise, surprise! He was in Montreal on a training course with his new company. Could we get together for an evening?

Delighted to have Clark in my home again, but this time three thousand miles further east, I learned that he was being trained as a salesman for a pharmaceutical corporation. What was a psychology major doing that for?

Clark related his adventures since the previous spring. In the summer, as usual, he worked for the park district, went to night school for a course in TESL and gained a certificate in Teaching English as a Second Language so that he could travel and work worldwide. By September, low in funds, he had decided to take a temporary job in sales; after answering every advertisement in the paper, he was accepted to sell insurance. The first day he made $170. But he became disillusioned with the job and the company as he met more and more customer complaints. Realizing that he enjoyed the selling but not the insurance, he left and decided to look for a job selling pharmaceutical products. Carefully researching various companies, their products, histories and developments, he wrote applications to twenty of them. A major company, with headquarters in Montreal, hired him.

I asked Clark how he felt about his new job. "I'm a little scared," he replied. "I'm dealing with a lot of drug names I've never heard of and can barely pronounce. And I've never committed myself to anything, except university, for any length of time. (And I still need one more course to graduate.) I really don't want to think that this is anything I'm going to be doing for a long period of time. Yet I believe this job is of God. I certainly prayed for direction. It's in hindsight that I can see how God has been good to me. He has provided. I haven't had any fantastic inspirations. I've had desires to do things, and I've followed some of my desires.

"It's really important for me to be in something that I think I should be in. But even that other job I had with the insurance company for a few months—I wouldn't say that was a mistake. That sales experience helped get me this job. And I really believe this isn't a mistake.

"I think it's important not to be set on doing one thing, because I think you can be really disappointed. And there might be some intermediate steps. By exploring a bit, you really might find you want to do something you hadn't even considered before. Life does take some funny bounces."

True. The only certainty is uncertainty itself. Though Christian workers are not necessarily less susceptible to misfortune than others, we do get the opportunity to delight in God's surprises, the unforeseen twists of the track that lead us in new directions. So we happily commit ourselves—our careers and our surprises—into God's hands, because only in his palms is there ultimate security. For that is where our names are written (Is 49:16).

Bad Surprises: When Tragedy Strikes

Henry was a Ugandan student in his second year of law at Kampala. Bright and articulate, a sincere Christian, he was ambitiously career conscious until a marauding gang of lawless armed soldiers burst into his house, senselessly killing several members of his family and demolishing the lower half of Henry's face with a blast from a shotgun.

With little more than immediate, self-administered first aid, Henry found his way to Kenya's Nairobi hospital. So devastating and deforming were his wounds that Henry became the celebrity subject of articles in learned medical journals. Christian friends in

Nairobi sent him to Amsterdam for further treatment. In Holland, a Christian missionary organization mounted a national campaign to raise sufficient funds to send him to a world-famous plastic surgery department in Montreal's Royal Victoria Hospital.

I visited him often in the hospital during the course of his six months of treatment, continuing the opportunity for friendship that had started when the bishop asked me to meet Henry at the airport. I saw him as horribly disfigured; scars and savage tears remained on his body where surgeons had borrowed flesh, bone and muscle to rebuild his jaw and neck. He could not speak or eat normally. Yet his eyes and the notebooks in which he wrote continually revealed his spirit as a flame of faith and courage.

We talked together one day of his future, Henry conversing by writing in his notebooks. We talked of how he would reshape his devastated life, of careers and work. He said he would never return to Uganda; he could never return to studying law. He had no idea what he could do, in fact. Where could he ever find useful and satisfying employment? The brutal surprise of the shotgun had destroyed more than just his lower face.

However, the brave determination of his spirit overrode the scribbled words on the pad. "As a human being," he wrote, "the accident was a terrible blow to my future. But spiritually this accident made my life change a lot, and my heart is a lot richer in faith. I never had patience at all with circumstances before the injury; but today I can look at bad things with an optimistic mind.

"I feel mine is like the story of St. Paul. . . . The important thing is this. I had friends in Uganda, very many in fact; but now I have friends in every continent. Wherever I go, it is easy to find a welcoming hand. It never was like this, and I don't think it would have been this way if the Lord hadn't used me as he did."

Intended careers may have to be shelved because of tragic surprises. The ballerina contracts multiple sclerosis; the football player loses a leg in a car crash; the business major has to return home to a prolonged family crisis, and is left with no space for pursuing his own career which had started with such promise. Examples of life-changing crises are easy to find.

I do not believe accidents and surprises of the tragic kind are sent willfully and deliberately by God. God did not have Henry's face blown off merely to teach him patience. Rather, destructive events are concomitant with our world's evil and, as with all evil, have their source and cause in the deliberations of Satan. Until the new heaven and the new earth come, Christians in the old territory will still be liable to disease and destruction, the surprise of the shotgun. Although that initial scream of anguish "Why me, O Lord?" will in this world remain unanswered (and therefore remain anguish), a subsequent question must be asked: *What now,* O Lord?" To that question, there are answers.

A person damaged by life's surprises must probably change his or her vocational plans out of sheer necessity. The invitation to bitterness, despair and jealousy will be strong. Even courageous Henry winced at the news of his younger brother's graduation as an electrical engineer, for in the normal run of events his own graduation would have preceded his brother's. But Henry turned aside the invitation to nurse his hurt, declaring, "But I'm glad of his success. His success is mine too."

Even the devastatingly surprised person may choose to work, to progress, to achieve in an area hitherto never dreamed of. The latest news of Henry is that he is in college in Kenya studying accounting. Joni Eareckson developed a totally new career for herself as a painter and author when a swimming accident left her paralyzed. She learned, after her bitter surprise, to hold the paintbrush in her mouth![7]

That is the choice for those hurt and disabled by life. You take a different path, a new and surprising one. But God is there. He is the God of all choices and all paths, no less present at that turning back there, off a little to the left, than at the obvious one up front to the right that you were intent on.

God's people are with you on these paths, too. You cannot conquer tragic circumstances in solitude. Disasters cannot be fought solo, as a David to a Goliath. You will want the help of professional counseling, vocational guidance, rehabilitative therapy, the caring support of family, friends and the church—the whole Christian community. The experience of others teaches us that trauma can be conquered. In God there is strength and creativity to rebuild a life of useful work.

Job Satisfaction

An elusive quality, satisfaction. In *The Beggar's Opera* Macheath says to Lucy Lockit, "I am ready, my dear Lucy, to give you satisfaction—if you think there is any in marriage."[1] I find something sadly prophetic about that comment; two and a half centuries after this work was written a husband and wife fully satisfied in their marriage is still a rarity. But what of contentment in careers? Are there any alternatives to humdrum? Who of us, like the dwarves in Walt Disney's *Snow White,* can march to work with a merry song?

"I can't get no satisfaction": these words from a Rolling Stones song epitomized the hedonistic despair of the seventies. But the phrase could well describe many people's contemporary experience with their work. For thousands of workers, work provides little or no satisfaction. It is the tedium and monotony of attaching the same old hinge to the same old door on the same old car on the same old assembly line. It is the despair of meaninglessness: mountains of paperwork or data cards, apparently vital to the maintenance of the corporation but in and of themselves meaningless. It is the self-demeaning task of working below one's capacities; of routine lab assignments that never offer scope for challenge, imaginative problem solving or self-directed research; of jobs that reduce the Ph.D. scholar to the role of mindless technician.

A Princeton research team found that up to eighty per cent of working Americans are in jobs that do not make use of their talents.[2] The horror of sameness, the no-future prediction that today's tasks will last till retirement, casts a wide shadow.

How to Succeed in Business without Really Trying

The optimistic, iconoclastic but financially expansionist 1960s gave rise to great optimism among people with respect to their careers, and the musical comedy title "How to Succeed in Business without Really Trying" fitted the ethos perfectly. With so much opportunity and scope in those days, you didn't even have to try to succeed. It was a winner's world, and every player was a winner.

By the early 1980s, however, the mood had changed. The economic recession meant cutbacks; governments reduced or eliminated subsidies; private companies went bankrupt daily; huge national corporations laid off senior staff and froze their hiring. Opportunities were severely limited. Few could succeed at all, and only then by hard work and massive doses of "luck."

With such an outlook for graduates and job seekers, what chance is there that today's prospective employees will have the luxury of being able to choose, and choose carefully, a career pattern that will satisfy them for a whole working life? Has the whole notion of job satisfaction had its life breath snuffed out by a drastically reduced job market? Even if job markets open as the recession turns around, are there jobs that will fulfill our expectations? Has career contentment gone the way of the Edsel and the five-cent Coke?

We discussed in chapter two the emotional load that a career is supposed to carry and decided it was too weak an ideal to fulfill all our criteria for success and satisfaction. A career cannot, indeed ought not, be a substitute for family love, friendship, marriage, childrearing, identity or God himself. Jesus is clear in his directive that we are not to give ourselves to money-oriented careers as slaves to a master. It is God alone that we must serve (Mt 6:24). Yet our work is a major element of our lives and one in which we surely need to find some sort of fulfillment and pleasure.

Does all the bad news mean that a realistic Christian contemplating a career must jettison all hope of job satisfaction, conform to monetary realities and accept any job she can get with thankfulness and stoicism? Though I grant the logic of answering yes, that somehow disturbs me. I think it foreshortens and inhibits the gifts of God in terms of his guidance and the pleasurable satisfaction that comes from being in his will in all things. Work is God's invention, designed for the pleasure of his creatures, and necessary to their fulfillment as unique individuals and as a species. "God has designed each of us to perform certain work and it's only when we perform that work that we're fulfilled."[3]

But First...
All of us operate at work on two levels. There is, of course, the level of task performance: going into the office, setting up the word processor and beginning to type the reports. But underlying the performance of the task itself is our fundamental attitude to our work, the way in which we view or perceive the task at hand. It is important that we learn first to find satisfaction at that deeper level, the level of attitude.

Rick was a student from Victoria, British Columbia, who had moved to Eugene, Oregon. He was eager to complete his M.S. in therapeutic recreation and then to race ahead into a doctorate and a brilliant career in research and teaching. The years in Oregon, however, were disastrous spiritually, financially and vocationally. Only the strength of a good marriage kept him sane. Eventually Rick realized the cause of his deep dissatisfaction: he was operating along the track of selfish ambition, with only the energy of his own human strength to pull the train.

In a recent letter he wrote,

God has confronted me with my selfish ambition. Jeremiah 45:5 —"Should you then seek great things for yourself? Seek them not." God has also opened my eyes to the shortsightedness of my planning. I was seeking something that was enjoyable and mean-ingful in *this* world and would result positively in *my* glory. Well, God has now changed my heart to a point where I just want to use all my abilities, skills, experience and uniqueness to *his* glory, to further *his* kingdom. I now have an eternal perspective.

From the satisfaction of that spiritually mature understanding, Rick is now continuing to work and build a career in counseling —without a Ph.D.

The inner contentment with oneself, one's identity, one's ambi-tions, is the crucial prerequisite to finding satisfaction in any sphere of life. For a Christian that inner contentment comes from God. We know whose we are and whom we serve. If, as you read this, you know only dissatisfaction at work—the nagging, discordant friction of unhappiness—realize that the battle might have to be fought at a deeper level first. Victory in the sphere of attitude can be the pre-lude to victory in the world of performance.

What Is Job Satisfaction?

Job satisfaction is not measured by the number of "WOWs" you exclaim each day, the desire with which you sprint to the office every Monday morning, the chances of meeting your future hus-band or wife at conferences, or the "per diem" allowance they give you for the week's trip to Minneapolis. Rather it touches quieter bases, answering more thoughtful needs.

Does your job seem spiritually right? Do you have the genuine sense that it is of God? That you are living in obedience to his will by working there? That your work-world parallels and harmonizes with your spiritual world? Are you, as Paul would say, *in Christ* in the office? Or, to get at the same point with a different question, are you basically the same person at work as you are at home or at church? Is there a spiritual consistency to your whole world? If you can answer a basic yes to these and similar questions, you have the beginnings of and foundation for job satisfaction.

I am convinced that the principles of satisfaction in the realm of work are identical to those in any other realm. The Christian thesis that "we find no rest until we find our rest in thee, O Lord" applies to vocation also.[4] Satisfaction, at its deepest, is akin to rest. Therefore any job satisfaction we are to feel or receive must be built on this spiritual foundation, that we do our work because we believe God has called us to do it. That calling is not only to jobs that have a definite Christian content (ministry, medicine or mission), and it does not necessarily come by visions or voices. But in every job we do, we need the quiet conviction that we are there in answer to God's call.

Can you function in your job with pride, respect and pleasure? Job satisfaction means taking a certain pride in your effort, your employer and your fellow employees. No satisfaction can be had if the thought of your work fills you with shame, or if you have nothing but a sneer for those around you on the shop floor. Ideally, you should build self-respect as you do your work, paralleled by respect for the purpose and end result of the whole group's labor. Satisfaction means, too, that a basic pleasure should stem from your work. This doesn't mean "every day is a gas, man!" or that you dance around every customer or client in an ecstasy of vocational vamp. But simply and regularly, your work should please you.

Is there a sense of growth in your job? Is there a career pattern which, as it develops, will increasingly challenge and stretch you so that you come close to fulfilling your potential over the years? Can you look forward to a "professional peak" at an appropriate time? A lifelong career should allow for vocational development to match your human maturation, so that growing through the years from age twenty-five to forty-five corresponds to a growth in responsibility and privilege at work.

Now That I Know What It Is, How Do I Get It?
Job satisfaction comes through good opportunities, good decisions, some hard work and a lot of goodly obedience to God.

Obviously an element of what this world calls luck may lead to a good job offer. Yet even so (and ignoring the theological problems that lie behind the notion of luck or fate), you can increase those chances of a good offer. "You've got to be willing to step off in faith," write Miller and Mattson, coauthors of *Finding a Job You Can Love,* "though in directions that maybe aren't conventional."[5] Energetically getting around the employment scene can help.

The organist at our church in Montreal is an outstanding musician and one of the few women who professionally conduct symphony orchestras. However, it is extraordinarily difficult to maintain a steady income in the uncertain world of classical music. So she started to think of alternate careers. She realized that she had, of all things, a lingering interest in the stock market. She signed up for a course in personal finance offered by a private foundation. On completion she took the optional test and scored the highest mark ever! The teacher promptly offered her a job in a brokerage firm, and within days she received another invitation to work. This is what I call energetically (and creatively) getting around the employment scene.

Recall how Clark tried to pry open some good opportunities. He had decided to become a pharmaceutical sales representative.

I went down to the library in Vancouver and looked up every company, got all the addresses in Canada. I found out a little bit about each company. I made out a résumé and a cover letter, and I sent off letters to everyone, about twenty different companies. Also, I just looked at the newspaper a lot. The job that I've got now, that was through the newspaper.

One thing I did at the interviews was important—I made sure I was really well prepared. Before the interview, I went down to the library, to the business section again, and looked up each company, and I think that's what impressed the company about me. I read how much money they made last year, what their products were, what new research they were doing, how the company was founded, who runs it, and a lot of background stuff.

I got responses from four companies. One from Calgary pretty well offered me a job after an interview. Another from Vancouver gave me an offer too. It was a toss-up right until the end which one I'd choose. I'm not qualified for the present job. They wanted someone with a strong science background and I'm a psychology major. But I got over this by the fact that I had researched the company.

"Opportunity knocks": so the cliché goes. But it knocks louder and more often for those who are actively seeking it. Of course it takes time and energy, and you can expect to spend days in libraries collecting data, days in the living room writing letters. But knocking on hundreds of doors certainly increases the odds of having one open. It is part of the route that can lead toward satisfaction.

Second, you need to make good decisions about choosing or accepting a job. This means that you might even have to say no to some offers. It is tempting, out of panic or despair, to accept the first offer that comes along. But a job has to be more than just a job if it is to bring satisfaction. Therefore be patient when necessary, and try to choose wisely, keeping in mind the components of satisfaction discussed earlier. Certainly, be sure to obtain as much information as you can about any situation. What exactly is the job? Who really owns this company? What are the implications of this job? Where does it lead immediately and ultimately? Choose prayerfully; choose well; seek counsel from wise and knowledgeable friends.

Finally, are you making job choices out of an ongoing lifestyle of obedience to the lordship of Jesus Christ? Some obvious features will tell you that there can be no satisfaction in certain job situations. Will it compromise your witness to Jesus? Will it compromise your morality? Will you have to lie and cheat to survive? Is the whole outfit crooked? Will you have to hide your Christian faith to get the job and then keep it? Will you be ashamed to let your friends know where you work?

Ask yourself questions also from the positive perspective: Does this job appear to be the answer to a specific prayer? Has the offer come in such a way that you can sense the guidance of the Holy Spirit? Do wise and just Christian friends share your sense of rightness about it? Is there a touch of the glory of God about it all?

You can actually, and most positively, expect the guidance of

God to lead you into job satisfaction. Would he omit the gift of his pleasure in one of the most important realms of your life? It is God's will to guide you—the unique you, your gifts, talents, interests, skills and qualifications—into satisfaction, to a work that fits you with the satisfying perfection that is typical of the Creator.

We are children of light, walking in the light (1 Jn 1:5-7). And that light shines on our work, helping us in our choices, tasks and relationships, bringing in that holy satisfaction.

The writer of Ecclesiastes should have the last word, for he knew at least one of the secrets of satisfaction at work. "There is nothing better for men than to be happy and do good while they live. That every man may eat and drink, and find satisfaction in all his toil—this is the gift of God" (Eccles 3:12-13). Would a loving Father withhold that gift from us?

Church and Career

Throughout this book I have assumed that you, the reader, are a member of a church fellowship, the primary Christian community. That is why I have regulary alluded to seeking counsel from Christian friends, talking matters over with a deacon, elder or minister. I have assumed that none of us lives or acts in defiant isolation. Rather, because the teaching of biblical Christianity makes it clear that all believers are members of Christ's body, and because the only effective way to live out that membership is by a visible presence in a visible congregation, I assume that you are a part of a local church.

I might be wrong, though. In that case this chapter could well provoke guilt . . . or longing. But for most of you, I am sure the assumptions are correct. Your church life has been supportive and encouraging. As you have wrestled with the perplexities of contemporary society, its uncertain economics, its rivalries, competitiveness and furious pace, you have known the guiding hand and steadying presence of your church fellowship.

However, some of you are going to find that the choice of a certain job entails a move to a new city or even a new country. You have to say good-by to your family and church to take that new position as a computer programmer in Ohio, dental receptionist in Seattle or petroleum engineer in Saudi Arabia. Leaving a good church that has been a home to you can be traumatic, accentuating the risk and anxiety that already plague you at the thought of your new position. How will you find a new church to replace the old one?

Finding a Church Home

In the syndicated cartoon strip "Shoe" the junior eagle, Skyler, delivers papers in the same way a fighter pilot shoots rockets. Approaching the favored house at a low-level dive, adjusting goggles with dramatic flair, he releases the tightly rolled newspaper at exactly the right moment to score a more-or-less direct hit on the front porch ... or an indirect hit on the front garden, the house next door, the roof, the swimming pool. His whole approach to delivering papers consists of these dangerous and inaccurate raids and sorties on unsuspecting householders.

Inevitably he has his problems. Occasionally he overshoots, or misses completely, or endangers his own life by crashing into chimneys. Anxious about the errors in his accuracy, he seeks guidance from a friend, a scientific type who promises to make an infallible heat-seeking apparatus that he can attach to each newspaper so that it will home in on its target. The gadget is good—too good, in fact. On his first approach with the paper-cum-missile, the heat-seeking technology works so well that everything—paper and bird, goggles and helmet—is swept ineluctably down a chimney from which smoke is curling. Ah well, the principle was good.

What we need in our search for a new church home is a comparable church-seeking device. (Perhaps Skyler might be selling his cheap.) We want to find our way unerringly to the right local church. But so many times new Christians in town just can't find a church anywhere, or at least not a good church. I suspect that the error is in the guidance system itself, the person. Many people with a new job seem to have almost casually thrown off the responsibility of attaching themselves to a fellowship. They have grown cold, become solos. The pleasures and duties of their new job have clogged not only their church-seeking system, but perhaps even their desire to look for a church home.

Christians who are transferred or who relocate of their own will might go about the business of homing in on the saints in several ways. Let's look at a few as our man Alan considers the options.

Alan is wildly excited. He's just landed his first, full-time, career-oriented job. On the strength of regular paychecks to come, he bought a new car (though suitably modest as befits a junior accounting assistant), which he has driven, with all his worldly goods packed therein, to the new town where he's going to work. Away from home, independent, free, ready to make his own way in the commercial world, he is wondering what to do on the first Sunday morning. Lonely, he decides to head off for church and begin a long-lasting, divinely guided, satisfying membership in a local community of dynamic believers, where he'll meet this fantastic Sunday-school teacher on a moonlit church picnic, and the world will be his.

Now, at that moment of indecision around 10:15 A.M. on the Sunday morning, Alan must think fast.

Same again, please. Perhaps Alan has a distinct loyalty to a denomination. As far back as he can remember, Alan has been a Baptist. He had some great times with his Baptist church back home, and he's genuinely committed to the Baptist way of doing things (although right now as he ponders the advertisements on the religious page of the Saturday paper, he wishes he could remember which conference his church belonged to. . . . How did there get to be so many different types of Baptists!). Taking a liking to one advertisement which offers a huge Sunday school (where there's kids, there's teachers), he jumps into his Tercel and drives off.

No one's looking: change now. Alternatively, Alan might be the kind of Baptist (or Mennonite or Lutheran or anything) who has just been waiting for a chance to change churches. Patiently living under the authority of family, habit or campus peers, he has bided his Baptist time until the moment when he would be free enough, and anonymous enough, to change denominations. Taking a deep breath, wide-eyed at the prospect of a totally different Sunday morning experience, Alan deliberately chooses a church far from his own style and excitedly enters the forbidden doors of . . . a Pentecostal tabernacle!

Yellow-pages roulette. In another town, another Alan, who never really thought about this business of finding a new church in a new town, is playing the dangerous game of yellow-pages roulette. Where else do you find a church than in the phone book? That's where everything else is . . . chairs, cheese and chimneys.

With finger-licking haste, he spins the yellow pages, letting his fingers do the walking until they stop by the largest and most attractive advertisement. Subconsciously equating size of ad with quality of church, he feels himself drawn to one that promises "gran' singin', gran' worshipin' and gran' prayin' " (yes, it really is spelled like that). Road map in hand, Alan walks off downtown to find it.

Drive and pray. With all the sincerity in the world, our Alan might have tried another ploy. Believing in the personal guidance of the Holy Spirit, as all Christians do, Alan decides to rely on nothing else. He gets into his Tercel, puts it in gear and drives around, following hunches and fuzzy feelings and dead ends and roadblocks until he knows, *he just knows,* that the church he's driving past is the one for him. He feels good about it. He's genuinely believed in guidance; he's put his faith into practice; he's submitted to God and trusted him for the answer. The only problem is that it's already 11:40 and the service is half over.

College fellowship nostalgia. Perhaps there is another scenario for graduates. This time our Alan is ex-president of his university campus group. The year before, he was vice president; and the year before that he was evangelism coordinator and delegate to the National Student Leaders' Conference. He loves campus work, thought for a while of joining staff, starting a graduate fellowship, or trying to get elected to the national board of a campus organization.

Eventually, with great reluctance, he took his farewell of his university group; they presented him with a cassette player and some John Stott tapes as a "token of their affection and appreciation for all that he had given them since his first year on campus" and promptly elected him "Inter-Varsity Man of the Decade."

It is now his first year off campus. In his new-apartment loneliness, his heart almost physically aches for his friends back at university. Hardly knowing what he's doing, he drives up to the campus of the college in his new town. Could there by chance be an IVCF meeting there this Sunday morning? A mission perhaps? A special summer-school fellowship group that goes together to a church, then picnics together, with sightseeing in the afternoon and a home Bible study at night in a friendly staffer's house?

Alan feels bad. He knows he isn't a student anymore, that he's got to grow up and make that transition between university and work that will withdraw him, like a reluctant tooth, from the safety and comfort of a student group. But so strong is his nostalgia for the university Christian fellowship that he cannot bring himself to go alone into a new church role ("So you're not a student, eh?"), and he drives aimlessly, nostalgia flooding, fighting his troubled conscience.

Grapevine rumors. Alan can't quite put his finger on it, but he knows that he met a girl once from this town at a Christian retreat, who told him of a fabulous church where all the keen, young Christians went. It was very informal, very alive; they had super music leaders, a team which did liturgical dance and skits, and a preacher who had written three of Alan's favorite books. But which church was it? Favorite books: that's the answer! Look on the back cover and see if it tells where the author comes from.

Frantically (it's past 10:30 now), Alan rips open carton after carton of unpacked books till he finds the one he wants. Yes, it does say: St. Paul's Episcopal, on Grosvenor. Where's Grosvenor? He grabs his map and checks the index. Oh no, it's all the way across town. Never mind, better late than never. And off Alan dashes.

Forget it! Then there's Alan in a different mood. Alan is exhausted by so much newness; by chasing down and setting up his apartment, completing forms for a medical card, license plates, dental plans and pension scheme; by studying the files for his first week's work; by meeting all the new faces in the office. Weakened by all the emotional pressure of being alone and neophyte, Alan cannot quite arouse enough energy to go to church this morning.

Nothing serious, folks. It's not a lifetime failure. He'll go next week. In fact, that will be better—give him time to look around, get organized, choose a proper church. Besides, first things first; he'd better get to know the city first. So what about a brunch somewhere and a little get-acquainted drive around town . . .

All these scenarios illustrate various ways in which typically, by my knowledge of people who changed jobs and locations, and by memory of my own moves, Christians who are new in town set off for their first Sunday in church. Some of these methods have their own merit (loyalty to a denomination is a fine quality), while others are frankly suspect. However, there is a "yet more excellent way"; and that starts with a biblical understanding of what a church is, the part that you are called to play in it, and how that all relates to work.

What Has Church Got to Do with Work?

If you are a Christian, then your church is crucial to the role work will play in your life.

Perhaps you can use the expertise, equipment and experiences of work to augment the work of the gospel through your church. You might find that church is a forum of activity where you can compensate for the stifling lack of creativity or fulfillment at work. Church will encourage you when problems plague, cool you when arguments heat, lift your spirits when gloom depresses, and generally keep you spiritually tuned up like a friendly mechanic.

From a descriptive point of view, the people who gather together and call themselves a church are identifiable in several ways. The biblical information comes from the book of Acts and the epistles of St. Paul, founder of many churches and a man whose work constantly took him into new locations.

First, churches were groups of people who met together weekly (sometimes daily) to commemorate the resurrection of Jesus. They were men and women who had come to a personal faith in Jesus of Nazareth as Messiah and Christ, Savior and Lord. They were baptized in his name and in the power of the Holy Spirit. As these churches expanded, as new churches resulted from the mission of the first-century Christians, the concept of an individual, concrete and localized church became a reality. Thus Paul could write to the church at Ephesus, for example, and St. John could write about the church at Smyrna.

Second, we know that these churches regularly celebrated what we now call Holy Communion, or the Eucharist, or the Lord's Supper. They broke bread together and shared a cup of wine as a sacramental memory of the Last Supper and as an anticipation of Jesus' coming again. This rite seems to have been the central act of their liturgy.

Third, the church met to listen to the apostolic preaching and teaching. There was an instructional intent to the services; new believers were catechized. Obviously, given the astronomic growth of the church, more than the original apostles engaged in teaching. Yet there was always the clear, unbroken link between Jesus' teaching and the instruction in doctrine in each church.

Fourth, the churches were centers of social aid. The poor who were in fellowship were supported through collections and distribution of money. Those in material need were cared for. Last, the churches prayed constantly. The people demonstrated the Spirit's gifts, binding themselves together in the Spirit's greatest gift, love.

The churches were never perfect. In no place, neither Corinth nor Jerusalem, could you have found an elite, superior band of morally perfect, absolutely united, impeccable disciples of the Lord Jesus. To read Paul's epistles is to understand that the churches he founded, visited and nursed were invaded by strife, animosity, rivalry, moral disobedience and apathy. Though the ideal of the church

138

(the people who are called out of society to be the people of God) calls for perfection, the reality is something less. The church is made of men and women who are in the process of being transformed into the likeness of Christ but who do not yet claim to have arrived (2 Cor 3:18).

Find a Good Church and Join It

Alan (remember Alan?) connects with history that very first Sunday morning when he makes his decision about which church to attend. Granted that it takes time to take the pulse of a church, he must nevertheless know the measure of a New Testament church so that he can judge the integrity and orthodoxy of his new one. All churches must be measured against the theology of the Scripture. I am afraid that we can no longer simply take the labels on the notice board outside a church at face value. The word *Christian* and the word *Church* are being distorted in violent ways in many of our cities, towns and villages.

If a group of people purport to be a church and yet bear no resemblance to any of the features of the New Testament church, their claim must be judged false. Again, we need to beware of the labels. Simply because a church is listed as the "Original Apostolic Witness Church of Biblical Inerrancy and Total Faith in Downtown Detroit," it does not necessarily follow that it is any of those things. The memory of Jonestown haunts us still. So perhaps the laid-back "Spring Heights Community Church" is more quietly faithful to the mark. Avoid those "churches" which never have the Lord's Supper, or biblical preaching, or prayer, or which never exhibit koinonia love, or which have their authority invested in a single, power-hungry individual.

I can not overemphasize how important it is, from a vocational point of view, to join a church when your job has caused you to move to a new location. Few support groups are able to operate with the quality of assistance that a church offers. That quality is, after all, divine.

What is a good church? A good church will exhibit those fundamental characteristics of New Testament fellowship groups: regular public meetings in an identifiable location, the sacraments of baptism and communion, regular biblical teaching, the education of children and new believers, evangelism, social service, and a recognition of the Spirit's presence in worship.

Some qualities of a good church are less objective; they are part of an ethos, an ambience. If a church genuinely worships from its heart, with enthusiasm, energy, creativity and sheer fun, that will be evident. If a church carries a sort of corporate humility, realizing its own inadequacies, errors, misunderstandings and imbalances, that too is a healthy and tangible trait. If a church is warm and friendly, open to newcomers without suffocating them ("Hi, Alan! How would you like to come to lunch?"), obviously involved with the lives of its community, then it is bearing the fruit of a good church.

So you find a good church and join it. But what happens if you cannot find a good church? What do you do then?

When to Join a Bad Church

If we hold too high a standard for the new town churches, we might find that they all fall short. Few churches will measure up to the biblical ideal. (Did any of the New Testament ones, consistently?) If we arrive in town clutching our dear memories of the Superchurch we left behind, perhaps again the new ones will fail to make the grade. If you intend to join a church *only* if the singing is Spirit filled always, or *only* if the preaching is at least at the John Stott-Urbana level, or *only* if they serve Mocha Java in the lounge after everything, or *only* if they have really pretty Sunday-school teachers, then you show yourself to be a spoiled brat. Be flexible with your standards of measurement. Let your definition of "good" stretch a little.

If, however, a church is bad because it is cultish, immoral, extremely authoritarian or patently unbiblical, then avoid it like the plague (which is, perhaps, what it indeed is). Cherish no ambitions about single-handedly renewing or purging such an outfit. There is something devilish (and that might be more than a figure of speech) about a godless group of people who call themselves a church, and you should have no truck with that.

A much more likely situation is one in which the church you are considering joining is bad because it is stumbling or faltering, that it is weak rather than bad. It has a tired pastor or poor preacher, no young people, a power-hungry organist, a pedantic senior sidesman, a vacuum of outreach, a glory that resides totally in the past. Such churches are not bad in the sense in which I am using the word in this chapter. They are not apostate. They simply need help. In that case, it could be that God is calling you to be that very help.

If you choose to join a church like this, your intent will be somewhat different. So will your welcome. It will take longer to fit in and feel at home. You will have to carry your own enthusiasm with you when you enter; you will more often be the "Hi-er" than the "Hi-ee." Alternatively, the people—all nineteen of them—will suffocate you with their needs, welcoming you as the hero sent to deliver, urging you to take on the Sunday school, the youth club, the choir, everything, by next Sunday.

You might find after only two weeks that the Sunday morning service is slow and dull, that the preaching is shallow, that there is no life. But I challenge you to consider God's call that you invest yourself in the life of this church, that you, with all your energy, giftedness, youth and rich spiritual understanding, suffer temporarily the loss of great singing and great fellowship in order to be used by God as an agent of renewal.

Diane Dadian's amusing but accurate article in *HIS* (June 1983), highlights this problem. A newly graduated student, Bill (I thought they were all called Alan), has transferred to Smalltown, U.S.A., to begin his first job. On the first Sunday he goes to the local church (the only option in Smalltown) where he unhappily finds himself stuffed between the old ladies and the children, between a fourteen-minute pastoral prayer and a semiliterate sermon. Diane reckons that Bill has three options: he can give in to discontent, run away or adjust. Some time later, a mellowed Bill has learned to love and receive love from the simple people of this church as he adjusts to their style.[1]

Sensitivity is an important factor in your adjustment. Avoid the impression that you are a Crusading Knight on a white charger, university degrees sweeping from your belt like chain mail, riding through the congregation with the Sword of Righteous Innovation in the Fist of Youth, hacking at ancient hymnbooks and tearing at traditions. They will not follow you if they see you as arrogant, impatient, critical or immature.

Somebody once said to a person seeking a church, "If ever you find a perfect church, don't join it; you'll ruin it." I like the tenor of that joke. It reminds me that the church is all too human, frail and weak because I am all too human, frail and weak. We must all learn to live with imperfections, others' and our own.

By several measures, the church at Corinth could have been counted a bad church. If you were a graduate from the University of Athens, newly arrived in Corinth for your job as export control officer for state antiquities, it is likely that you would have held back from joining the fellowship there. Such goings on! Sexual stuff, too—the very worst. And fighting? And rivalries? How could such a church have got a write-up in the New Testament? And yet it was to this church that Paul wrote, "We, . . . with unveiled faces all reflect the Lord's glory" (2 Cor 3:18).

Let's be patient with the so-called bad churches.

Three Families

When I arrived in Edmonton in 1967, with all my worldly goods packed into a green Volkswagen bug, I was totally unknown to the 300,000 residents. No one met me; no one cheered. My only securities were my teaching contract at a local high school and my determination to join a church as soon as possible.

I found from the newspaper the address and time of a large downtown Baptist church that looked good. Realizing that I would be late even if I did find the place, I pulled over and dropped into a small, almost anonymous Baptist church that I happened to be driving past.

That very first morning I met my Sunday-school teacher. Which
proves nothing, except that God is good. I never got to that downtown church, but I found a church family in the small fellowship
and found the partner to begin creating a home with.

In a sense we belong simultaneously to three family groups: the
family at home, the family at work and the family at church. In an
ideal world the three would form a harmonious triad of mutual support. In the reality of our fractured society, however, we are often
left with only the family at church.

How can our church family help us succeed in our work? The
church is the Christian body that reinforces the habits, attitudes
and actions that spring from godly righteousness. We know that we
should not lie or cheat; we know that we should not smoke dope or
sleep around. Yet it can be painfully lonely and too demanding to be
the only bearer of a Christian ethic in a work situation where everyone else (or so it seems) is cruel, crass or promiscuous. Only from
our church family can we be sure of understanding, comfort and
the prayer support to maintain us in godly righteousness.

The church family provides a home base from which equipment
is drawn to do the work of an evangelist—at work. Wherever we
are, whatever our job, whoever our colleagues, we are called by God
to be witnesses to what the Lord Jesus has accomplished. Again,
the training and encouragement we need comes from our church
family. It is impossible to function adequately at work as a Christian without the intimate fellowship that church provides.

So the church reinforces within us all that is godly. It can also
compensate for a job that is bitter, ugly or unfulfilling. The image
of Wednesday-night prayer meeting as a first-aid station, a place to
lick our wounds after three savage days in the trenches at work, is
a sad one; it is nonetheless accurate for many. We do get hurt at
work. We do get emotionally scarred. We are surrounded by hard
people with hard words ordering us to do hard tasks. Their sharp-
ness severs our nerves. I have often spent a pastoral hour listening
to a parishioner complain of abuse, unfairness and mockery at
work. In those cases, let us freely turn to the gentle love of our

brothers and sisters in Christ to salve the wounds. They augment the work of Jesus, who said, "Come to me, all you who are weary and burdened, and I will give you rest" (Mt 11:28).

Small-*m* Ministry

Many of us are familiar with that too-old-to-be-youth-group class called the College and Careers group. Current employment prospects are bleak enough to be forcing churches to add "and Unemployed" to this title.

What can churches do to help those who find themselves unemployed? Obviously, we can provide essential encouragement. Everlasting line-ups at employment centers, followed by everlasting bus rides to personnel offices, followed by everlasting "Sorry but no"s from managers, are so depressing. Regular support through prayer and sharing groups is essential. But there are more objective ways in which churches can help fend off the lack-of-money panic that afflicts wage earners when suddenly they're not anymore.[2]

Those still fortunate enough to be wage earners can pool an extra tithe (perhaps one-twentieth of their salary) to establish a fund for the continuing expenses of mortgage, medicine, insurance, telephone and utilities of those who have been laid off. Food and clothing can be distributed. The people of my church in Montreal rented a storefront for that purpose, to serve nutritious meals at fifty cents and to supply good used clothing for a dollar. A church in Detroit responded similarly to that city's 1980 recession.[3]

God calls few to professional, large-*M* ministry in the church. But he calls all of us to small-*m* ministry, that is, to use our treasure, time and talents in his service. We have talked of ways in which your church can reinforce godliness at work. But how can your work help support the life of your church?

Examples come to my mind immediately. Marlene works in a plastics factory and supplies materials for notice boards and children's work. Tim and Peter are computer programmers, and they have created a mailing list for our Anglican Youth Camp registrations, standardized menus, and printed a beautiful training manual. Reg is a financial analyst and has volunteered his time to pilot many churches through a missions phase. Jennie works for a broadcasting company; with her language skills she wrote radio advertisements for a crusade. Robert owns a cleaning company and has lent us some of his men and materials at advantageous rates. And so the list goes on. While careful to make sure that no commercial enterprise ends up unknowingly subsidizing the work of the church (that is plainly unethical), there are various ways in which individuals can use their business or professional expertise and resources to aid the mission of the church.

Although the days at work may seem spiritually stifling, or simply unconnected in any way with the march of the gospel, you may find a real outlet for your spiritual and even career energies through your local church. Openings for public school teachers may be few, but your teaching gifts can get exercise at church. It is volunteer leaders who carry the Sunday school, the youth group, the meals-on-wheels, the outreach center, the overseas missions connection. It is volunteers who create flow charts of five-year plans, prepare banquets and draw blueprints for the addition to the parish hall.

I think it was G. K. Chesterton who said that an atheist is a person with no invisible means of support. The church is, by design, a group of amateurs who *do* have an invisible means of support, the Lord Jesus himself. That invisible means of support is with us always, even—perhaps especially—at our place of work. He becomes, however, almost visible in the church, his body, where we work together at our mutual vocation of kingdom building.

Where Are They Now?

Two years have passed since we set out to track our eight Christian students through their last year at the University of British Columbia and into the work-world. By interviewing them monthly throughout their final year, I explored their activities and attitudes, their vocational Christianity-in-action, as they went through the process and pressure of deciding career entry points and finding that somewhat elusive job.

Well, how did they do? Who got what? A year has passed since they graduated. What are they actually doing?

Let's start with the married couple, Herb and Sandy.

Baby Bonus

The married couple is now a family of three. Baby Jordan complicated Sandy's vocational plans with his delightful arrival some five months after his mother graduated with a degree in forest genetics. (Herb's comment: "Considering who she's married to, she now has two babies to care for!") However, Sandy's debut into the career of motherhood has been so satisfying that a second child will come along soon.

Herb has not yet completed—or even really started—his thesis necessary for graduation, although his coursework for his B.S. in forestry has been tucked away. He is still working as a baggage handler for Canadian Pacific Air, while in the summer he joins his wife and mother-in-law in the domestic swimming pool business.

Herb and Sandy have achieved an enviable financial stability through his work at C. P. Air (they have, remarkably, bought a house), and it seems that Herb's university studies have been subordinated to the business of living. Yet his strong Christian commitment has not been compromised. He and Sandy are loyal members of a church fellowship and are involved in a vital small-group prayer and study, whose numbers include friends from their junior high-school days. In between caring for one baby and expecting another, Sandy helps an evangelistic Bible study group that reaches out to neighborhood women.

Though neither Herb nor Sandy has entered into the primary stages of a major career pattern, they are well established in perhaps the more important (and ultimately more satisfying) areas of life— in family love, in parenting, in establishing a home, and in vital Christian involvement with the community of Christ.

Bad Classes and Budget Cuts
Dear Mike:

Unfortunately, I received your Christmas letter somewhat late. Hence I am writing to you months later. As for what has been happening regarding my career . . . Well, here goes.

Last year I was indoctrinated into the teaching profession through ten months of intense frustration. I had a class of 26 grade-six pupils. It was a particularly difficult class, to say the least. I also taught grade-seven French and music, and grade-five music and art. The one saving grace (so to speak) was the choir, which I helped lead in conjunction with another teacher.

By May last year, the B.C. government began its first of a series of budget restraints on education. As a result, our school was one person overstaffed. An opportunity came for me to transfer to a slightly larger school and lead the music program there. Well, I figured it might be a welcome change, so I transferred.

I am presently teaching grade four. I trade off P.E. and science to teach grade-five music and grade-one French. I am enjoying my vocation a lot more now. The one drawback is that this school is in a rather transient area, and students transfer in and out on an all-too-frequent basis. Lately, more and more have been joining our class, so that my class size is 37 and still growing. Needless to say, that limits what I can do for individuals.

The teaching profession is undergoing great turmoil at the present, with 100 layoffs projected for our district next September. I have a permanent contract and am a classroom teacher (that is, not librarian or the like), so I shouldn't be one of the first to go.

This leads me to career plans for next year. I have been approached and have accepted a post teaching grade-six French immersion. Although I was somewhat reluctant at first, not being a native French Canadian, I am now quite excited. The job is still dependent on getting enough students to open up a new class. If all this falls into place, I will be going back to Montreal to take some courses on teaching immersion.

As for church, I have been attending Burnaby Christian Fellowship, a very large and lively congregation. I have been somewhat involved in a choir there, though little is organised in the way of a formal affair. I was going to a home fellowship group, but that fizzled out.

Well, I'd better stop writing and start mailing if I want you to get this before next Christmas.

Take care,

In Him,

Glenda

Two different teaching jobs in her first two years (plus another change coming up) have meant a difficult career launch for Glenda. With the "double whammy" of bad classes and budget cuts, she must feel more like a ball in a pinball machine than a person leisurely and thoughtfully establishing a career base.

She's tough, though, and has not let frustration and difficulty defeat her. She's garnering also the rewards of endurance. Her obvious skills in music and French allow her to move toward specialty situations which have produced two benefits: she has not been laid off, and she increasingly gets to choose jobs which will bring satisfaction and pleasure. Particular ability—in this case the fruit of circumstance (she was brought up in the bilingual city Montreal), aptitude and industry—pays off. The first to go and the last hired are the generalists who can offer nothing extra.

If you are planning to enter an established profession like teaching, learn from Glenda. Magnify a specialty; develop skills and experience in it; and be prepared for a difficult year or two initially.

A Kingdom Lawyer

Carol, the piano-playing biology major, is now in her second year of law, preparing to start her year of professional articling—as long as she graduates. And her letters give every indication that she will.

Carol has studied law with a consciously Christian motive and from a consciously Christian world view. This has led her into voluntary work at an L.S.L.A.P. office, which, although sounding rude, is actually a Law Students' Legal Aid Program for the poor and disadvantaged. She works in Vancouver's downtown eastside. Here's how she describes it:

> It's exciting in more ways than one. I enjoy talking to people, and the legal aspect of the clinic merely facilitates that.
>
> Occasionally, we get a few "real" legal problems and put some knowledge to use after having heard life stories from skid row. It's neat to see people as worthy of your time and care, however they may appear externally.

Undergirding all her study, overarching all her ambitions for the future, is her Christlike motivation to be "effective for the kingdom." What a great model for all of us as we enter our careers! No matter what our job may be, we are called to be living witnesses to what God has accomplished through Jesus. Therefore our daily ambition is to search for ways in which our work (mistakenly called secular employment) can be used to advance and highlight the presence of God's kingdom. For our work is our vocation. We are ambassadors for Christ, who said, "The kingdom ... has come upon you" (Mt 12:28).

Jesus Christ ushers in the kingdom, the rule of God in our hearts and lives. Our world of work has become an arena in which our performance advances or retards the presence of that kingdom. That is why a Christian law student like Carol is looking for ways in which her professional life can be "effective for the kingdom."

That Useful Undergraduate Degree

Steve is the second student of our group who is actually working in the field for which his undergraduate degree trained him, though his route to gainful employment was not as direct as it might have been. He took that deadly bypass, the way of the traveling salesman, forced into it by the panic of unemployment. Here's how Steve tells it.

> Well, two weeks of unemployment looked like eons, so I jumped at this advertisement wanting a salesman with a good agriculture background to develop the peat moss market. To make a long story short, I only lasted two and a half months before receiving the left boot of fellowship. Besides finding a cheaper way to market their product, the Head Honchos saw that I didn't possess that killer instinct of the seasoned salesman. I certainly learned a lot, not the least being that the traveling salesman's job is not for me!

Still smarting from that left boot, Steve applied for every job he found that fitted his education. Eventually he landed one, and he is now classifying various forest ecosystems in northern B.C. His employer is the Provincial Ministry of Forests, and his technical title is "pedologist" (that is, a soil scientist).

Steve is occasionally wistful about working more directly with people, the salt of the earth rather than the earth itself. He has some back-burner thoughts about working overseas—on foreign soil, one might say. He enjoys, though, the "containedness" of his job; he does not have to take it home with him at night, nor be burdened by emotional pressures. That leaves him free for church activities, social affairs, leisure and playing trombone in the Prince George symphony (not of recording fame). He's currently rehearsing Tschaikovsky's Fifth—"a real brassy affair, lots of trombone."

An Academic in Scotland

Rob was the student who professed an interest in teaching at the university level. Consequently, after graduating from UBC, he went to Calgary, Alberta, to do what he modestly called "a whole bunch of courses." The bunch included Latin, Greek, German and theology. From there he set his sights on a doctorate, and so the next problem was to choose a university and be accepted.

He chose the University of St. Andrews, in Fife, Scotland, partly because his family had some traditional connections with the place and partly because the level and focus of scholarship there was in conformity with his own aspirations. So Rob is pursuing the first year of an M.Phil. to lead into the doctorate. His thesis area will be Redaction Criticism of the Parables in Matthew 13.

Though the level of Christian fellowship leaves something to be desired (apparently those dour Scots still exist!), Rob is excited by his plans and satisfied with his progress.

And Then There Were Two

Thus far we've seen the careers of six of our UBC students. Two more remain. We have met Clark on several occasions. He continues his work as a pharmaceutical sales representative. But as of the moment of this writing, Sheila is untraceable. It seems that she has returned to Japan, where her parents are missionaries and where she was brought up. But I have no details.

I wrote in the introduction that we were all determined to relate honestly and straightforwardly our entry into the world of work. That we have done. Although not all have even yet entered into a firmly established career stream, all are still firmly involved in the major task of being disciples of Jesus Christ. All are operating out of a basic satisfaction and pleasure in life, in knowing God and in pursuing the tasks of their studies and employment. None has been lost, as Jesus might say. None is unemployed. None is depressed. None has given up the faith.

You Mean I Might Actually Get a Job?

In the delightful cartoon strip "Doonesbury," by Gary Trudeau, Mike and Zonk discuss work possibilities. Mike is a successful, mainstream middle-class student, moving easily and confidently from one life scene to another; whereas Zonk is a startlingly free individualist, a nonconformist who rebels against accepted codes and is frightened of making the inevitable compromise with society that graduation calls for.

DOONESBURY   by Garry Trudeau

Cartoon and dialog below are from Doonesbury, copyright, 1982, G. B. Trudeau. Reprinted with permission of Universal Press Sundicate. All rights reserved.

In the next strip, Zonk returns after spending a harrowing day among the recruiters.

Mike: Hey! He's back! How did it go?

Zonk: Listen, Mike, I have an idea. Let's break into the registrar's office and tamper with our records and make ourselves juniors again.

Mike: That bad, huh?

Zonk: Worse. One guy actually tried to give me a job. If I hadn't put down a fake name, I'd be employed right now!

Mike: You'd better sit down. You look a little shook up.

Zonk: You told me there weren't any jobs, Mike. You lied to me! The ironic humor of Trudeau's cartoon characters is delicious, and awfully close to the mark for some of us. Take heart from the funnies. There *are* jobs out there. You will get offered one; you will take it. And it will be good.

A Tale of Two Gardeners

Once upon a time, a man moved into a house close to the outskirts of a small town. He was a farmer, and he worked his hundred acres carefully and well, growing grain crops. But at heart he was a gardener of flowers.

Next to his house was some land that the town council owned. It lay fallow—neglected, overgrown and tangled with weeds. He petitioned the town council to allow him to buy the land for a garden. The councilors were reluctant to lose control of the lot but eventually acceded to his request.

For a whole year the man did nothing except prepare the land for growing flowers. He cleared all the debris and waste; he hacked away all the tangles and weeds. He dug the soil and manured it. Within three years he had turned that vacant plot into a dazzling array of flowers. Owing to his industry and care, flowers bloomed from the earliest spring days to the last fall frosts.

One day a new church minister walked by. Seeing the man working among the flowers, he stopped to talk. "How grateful you must be to God for the gift he has given you here in this beautiful garden," began the minister. And he continued in the same vein, saying how thankful the man must be for all the work that God had done in growing and bringing to blossom all the flowers. Surely the man's heart was filled with admiration for the wonders of God's work!

"Maybe," mused the man. "But you should have seen this land when God had it all to himself!"

Without God and his grace, we can produce nothing of lasting substance or permanent value. Yet without the labor of our hands and the work of our minds, few flowers would be blooming on the wastelands of our earth.

Appendix

General Resources for Designing a Career Plan

Bachhuber, Thomas D., and Hardwood, Richard K. *Directions: A Guide to Career Planning.* Boston: Houghton Mifflin, 1978.

Bolles, Richard. *What Color Is Your Parachute?* Rev. ed. Berkeley, Calif.: Ten Speed Press, 1978.

Bradley, John D. *Christian Career Planning.* Portland, Oreg.: Multnomah Press, 1977.

Cull, John G., and Hardy, Richard E., eds. *Career Guidance for Black Adolescents.* Springfield, Ill.: Charles C. Thomas, 1975.

Farnsworth, Kirk E., and Lawhead, Wendell H. *Life Planning: A Christian Approach to Careers.* Downers Grove, Ill.: InterVarsity Press, 1981.

Greco, Benedetto. *How to Get the Job That's Right for You.* Homewood, Ill.: Dow Jones—Irwin, 1975.

Haldane, Bernard. *Career Satisfaction and Success: A Guide to Job Freedom.* New York: Amacom, 1972.

Jameson, Robert J. *The Professional Job Changing System.* Verona, N.J.: Performance Dynamics, Inc., 1976.

Knight, David M. *How to Interview for That Job—and Get It!* Connersville, Ind.: News-Examiner Company, Inc., 1976.

Looking Ahead to a Career. Washington, D.C.: U.S. Department of Labor, 1975 (pamphlet).

Mattson, Ralph, and Miller, Arthur. *Finding the Job You Can Love.* Nashville, Tenn.: Thomas Nelson, 1982.

Pell, Arthur R. *The College Graduate Guide to Job Finding.* New York: Simon and Schuster, 1973.

Powell, C. Randall. *Career Planning and Placement Today.* 2nd ed. Dubuque, Iowa: Kendall/Hunt Publishing Co., 1978.

Reed, Jean, ed. *Résumés That Get Jobs.* New York: Arco Pub. Co. Inc., 1976.

Schein, Edgar H. *Career Dynamics: Matching Individual and Organizational Needs.* Reading, Mass.: Addison-Wesley Publishing Co., 1977.

White, Jerry, and White, Marry. *Your Job: Survival or Satisfaction?* Grand Rapids, Mich.: Zondervan, 1977.

Resources for Exploring Career Options

The Academy Catalog. Chicago, Ill.: International Academy of Merchandising and Design, Limited, 1978.

Allied Health Education Programs in Junior and Senior Colleges. Hyattsville, Md.: U.S. Department of Health, Education, and Welfare, 1975.

Allied Medical Education Directory. 8th ed. Chicago, Ill.: American Medical Association, 1979.

Bestor, Dorothy D. *Aside from Teaching English What in the World Can You Do?* Seattle, Wash.: Univ. of Washington Press, 1977.

Business Economics Careers. Cleveland, Ohio: National Association of Business Economics, 1975 (pamphlet).

Campus Life's Guide to Christian Colleges. Wheaton, Ill.: Youth for Christ, 1981.

Career Information for College Graduates. Bethlehem, Pa.: College Placement Council, Inc., 1976.

Career Opportunities: Community Service and Related Specialists. New York: Doubleday, 1975.

Claxton, Ronald H., and Lorenzen, Biddie. *The Student Guide to Mass Media Internships.* Boulder, Colo.: Intern Research Group, School of Journalism, Univ. of Colorado, 1979.

The College Handbook. New York: College Entrance Examination Board, 1975.

College Placement Annual. Bethlehem, Pa.: College Placement Council, Inc., n.d.

Dictionary of Occupational Titles. 4th ed. Washington, D.C.: Superintendent of Documents, U.S. Government Printing Office, 1977.

Education Directory: Colleges and Universities. Washington D.C.: U.S. Department of Health, Education, and Welfare, 1975.

Federal Career Directory. Washington, D.C.: Superintendent of Documents, U.S. Government Printing Office, 1976.

Guide to Federal Career Literature. Washington, D.C.: Superintendent of Documents, U.S. Government Printing Office, 1974.

Handbook of Trade and Technical Careers and Training. Washington, D.C.: National Association of Trade and Technical Schools.

Health Careers Planning Guide. Urbana, Ill.: Univ. of Illinois, 1976.

Johnson, Willis L., ed. *Directory of Special Programs for Minority Group Members: Career Information Services, Employment Skills Banks, Financial Aid Sources.* 2nd ed., Garrett Park, Md.: 1975.

Livesey, Herbert B. and Harold Doughty. *Guide to American Graduate Schools.* New York: Penguin, 1977.

Malnig, Lawrence R., and Morrow, Sandra L. *What Can I Do with a Major in . . . ?* Jersey City, N.J.: Saint Peter's College Press, 1975.

Manual of Training for Business and Industry. Scranton, Pa.: Intext, Inc., 1975.

Mitchell, Joyce Slayton. *I Can Be Anything: Careers and Colleges for Young Women.* New York: College Entrance Examination Board, 1978.

A Newspaper Career and You. Princeton, N.J.: Newspaper Fund, 1976.

Newspaper Internships for College Students. Princeton, N.J.: Newspaper Fund, 1978.

Occupational Outlook Handbook. 1976-77 ed. Washington, D.C.: Superintendent of Documents, U.S. Government Printing Office, 1976-77.

Prelaw Handbook. Washington, D.C.: Association of American Law Schools and the Law School Admission Council, (current year).

Schola, Nelle Tumlin, et al. *How to Decide: A Guide for Women.* New York: College Entrance Examination Board, 1975.

Shingleton, John D., and Frank, Phil. *Which Niche?* East Lansing, Mich.: John D. Shingleton and Phil Frank, 1969.

Taking Care of Business: Exploring Career Possibilities in Business (Highlights from a Forum for Undergraduate Black Students). Atlanta, Ga.: 1977.

Teal, Everett A. *The Occupational Thesaurus.* Vols. 1 and 2. Bethlehem, Pa.: Lehigh Univ., 1971.

Thain, Richard J. *The Managers: Career Alternatives for the College Educated.* Bethlehem, Pa.: College Placement Council, Inc., 1978.

Walker, John H., III. *Thinking about Graduate School: A Planning Guide for Freshman and Sophomore Minority College Students.* Princeton, N.J.: Educational Testing Service, 1974.

Westbrook, Bert W. *Career Development Needs of Adults.* Washington, D.C.: American Personnel and Guidance Association and The National Vocational Guidance Association, 1978.

Wiggs, Garland, ed. *Career Opportunities: Marketing, Business and Office Specialists.* New York: Doubleday, 1975.

Resources for Identifying Prospective Employers

Note: *Directories* are listings of organizations and executives. *Information* indicates an address to write to for advice on how to obtain additional directory information and possible job vacancies.

General Aids
Directories:

Graduate and Professional School Opportunities for Minority Students. 6th ed. Princeton, N.J.: Educational Testing Service, 1975-77.

Graduate Programs and Admissions Manual 1977-1979. Princeton, N.J.: Educational Testing Service, 1977.

Renetzky, Alvin, ed. *Directory of Internships, Work Experience Programs and On-the-Job Training Opportunities*, 1st ed. Thousand Oaks, Calif.: Ready Reference Press, 1976.

The College Handbook Index of Majors. New York: College Entrance Examination Board, 1977.

Information:

Angel, Juvenal L. *Directory of Professional and Occupational Licensing in the United States*. New York: World Trade Academy Press, Inc., 1970.

Encyclopedia of Associations. 10th ed. Vols. I and II. Detroit, Mich.: Gale Research Co., 1976.

Wasserman, Paul. *Encyclopedia of Business Information Sources*. 3rd ed. Detroit, Mich.: Gale Research Co., 1976.

Business and Industry
Directories:

The Becker Guide. Chicago, Ill.: Becker and Warburg-Paribas Group, Inc., 1975.

College Placement Annual 1978. Bethlehem, Pa.: College Placement Council, Inc., 1978.

The Executive's Corporate Handbook (Joseph Lloyd Corporation). Winnetka, Ill.: Joseph Lloyd Corp., 1975.

Salmon, Richard D. *The Job Hunter's Guide to Eight Great American Cities*. Cambridge: Brattle Publications, 1978.

Standard and Poor's Register of Corporations, Directors and Executives. Vol. 1. New York: Standard and Poor's Corporation, 1977.

Information:

Dun and Bradstreet, Inc., 666 Fifth Ave, New York, NY 10019. Publishes business directories.

Moody's Investors Service, Inc., 99 Church Street, New York, NY 10007. Publishes several manuals on business and industry.

Christian Professions
Information:

Christian Service Corps, 1509 16th Street N.W., Washington, D.C. 20000.

Intercristo, Box 9323, Seattle, WA 98109.

National Association of Evangelicals, 350 South Main Place, Carol Stream, IL 60187.

Yearbook of American and Canadian Churches. New York: Abingdon Press, revised and published annually.

Education
Directories:
Association of Christian Schools International, Directory. LaHabra, Calif.: ACSI, 1979.
Elliott, Norman F., ed. *Patterson's American Education.* Vol. 73. Mt. Prospect, Ill.: Educational Directories, Inc., 1977.
National Union of Christian Schools, 865 28th Street Southeast, Grand Rapids, MI 49508.
State Offices of Education usually publish a directory.

Government Jobs
Directories:
A Guide to Government Employment in the Midwest. St. Paul, Minn.: Midwest College Placement Council, 1976 (pamphlet).
Working for the USA. Washington, D.C.: U.S. Civil Service Commission, 1978 (pamphlet).
Information:
U.S. Civil Service Commission and Federal Job Information Center. See telephone directory under "United States Government" or obtain the toll-free number by calling 800/555-1212.

Overseas Employment
Information:
Opportunities Abroad for Teachers. Washington, D.C.: U.S. Department of Health, Education, and Welfare, 1977-78.
Schultz, Gordon F. *How to Get a Job Overseas with an American Firm or Affiliate.* Burbank, Calif.: Overseas Employment Guides, 1977.
————. *How to Get a Job Overseas with the United States Government.* Burbank, Calif.: Overseas Collegiate Research Institute, 1976.

Welfare and Service Agencies
Directories:
Haimes, Norma, ed. *Helping Others: A Guide to Selected Social Service Agencies and Occupations.* New York: John Day Co., 1974.
Moore, Michele, ed. *Public Welfare Directory.* Vol. 38. Washington, D.C.: American Public Welfare Assoc., 1977.
————. *National Directory of Child Abuse Services and Information.* 1st ed. Chicago, Ill.: National Committee for Prevention of Child Abuse, 1974.

Information:
Local Welfare Office—inquire about state and local directories for organizations
  providing human services.

Notes

Chapter 1: When I Was a Child

[1]"Stephen Jay Gould: L'homme qui va plus loin que Darwin," interview in *L'Actualité*, May 1983; my translation.

[2]*Gazette* (Montreal), 7 May 1983.

[3]William Barclay, *The Daily Study Bible*, vol. 1, *The Gospel of Matthew* (Edinburgh: St. Andrew Press, 1972), p. 402.

Chapter 2: After You Graduate

[1]R. W. Southern, *Western Society and the Church in the Middle Ages* (New York: Penguin Books, 1970), p. 278.

[2]"Life among the Boomies," *Saturday Night*, October 1979, p. 16.

[3]Kenneth Kantzer, "Can Christian Colleges Survive the Eighties?" *Christianity Today*, 16 September 1983, p. 8.

[4]Paul Vitz, *Psychology as Religion: The Cult of Self-Worship* (Grand Rapids, Mich.: Eerdmans, 1977).

[5]J. I. Packer, *Knowing God* (Downers Grove, Ill.: InterVarsity Press, 1973).

[6]C. S. Lewis, *The Voyage of the Dawn Treader* (New York: Macmillan, 1975), p. 81.

Chapter 3: Circling Around

[1]Kirk E. Farnsworth and Wendell H. Lawhead, *Life Planning* (Downers Grove, Ill.: InterVarsity Press, 1981).

[2]Intercristo, P.O. Box 33487, Seattle, WA 98133, is one of several agencies that will provide information regarding work in Christian ministries.

[3]Kantzer, "Can Christian Colleges Survive?" pp. 8, 10.

[4]"Where Are the Jobs of 1990?" (my translation), *L'Actualité*, September 1982, p. 49.

Chapter 4: What Is This Thing Called Work?

[1]W. Somerset Maugham, *The Explorer* (London: Heinemann, 1967), p. 43.

Chapter 5: There Are Christian Workers but Are There Christian Jobs?

[1]Brother Lawrence, *The Practice of the Presence of God*, trans. E. M. Blaiklock (London: Nelson, 1982).

[2]Matthew Arnold, *Culture and Anarchy* (Cambridge: At the University Press, 1932), p. 47.

[3]Laurence Shames, "Devil's Work," *Esquire*, July 1982; excerpted in *HIS*, June 1983, pp. 5-6.

Chapter 6: Choosing a More Challenging Way

[1]Tom Sine, *The Mustard Seed Conspiracy* (Waco, Tex.: Word, 1981), p. 147.

[2]Arthur Gish, *Beyond the Rat Race* (New Canaan, Conn.: Keats Publishing, 1973).

[3]Ronald Sider, ed., *Living More Simply* (Downers Grove, Ill.: InterVarsity Press, 1980).

[4]Ibid., p. 87.

[5]Ibid., p. 82.

[6]Quoted ibid., p. 13.

[7]Jonathan Baylis, *Interaction* (IVCF Canada), February 1984.

[8]Sine, *Mustard Seed Conspiracy*, p. 137.

[9]Richard Foster, *Freedom of Simplicity* (San Francisco: Harper & Row, 1981).

Chapter 7: Getting There from Here: Guidance

[1]Philip Yancey, "Finding the Will of God: No Magic Formulas," *Christianity Today*, 16 September 1983, pp. 24-27.

[2]*Julius Caesar*, act 4, sc. 3, 1.217.

[3]Packer, *Knowing God*, p. 98. I recommend all of chapter 11.

[4]Richard J. Foster, *Celebration of Discipline* (San Francisco: Harper & Row, 1978).

[5]Yancey, "Finding the Will of God."

[6]Bob Slosser, *Miracle in Darien* (Plainfield, N.J.: Logos Int., 1979).

[7]Jerram Barrs, *Shepherds and Sheep: A Biblical View of Leading and Following*

(Downers Grove, Ill.: InterVarsity Press, 1983), p. 92.

[8]M. Blaine Smith, *Knowing God's Will* (Downers Grove, Ill.: InterVarsity Press, 1979).

Chapter 8: When Guidance Goes Sour

[1]John White, *The Fight* (Downers Grove, Ill.: InterVarsity Press, 1976), chap. 8.

[2]Susan Cooper, *Silver on the Tree* (New York: Atheneum, Aladdin Books, 1979), p. 176.

Chapter 9: Surprises

[1]*L'Actualité,* April 1982, p. 90.

[2]Jn 2:1-11; 5:8-10; 6:9-14; 11:38-44. See also Mt 19:25; Mk 2:12; Lk 7:16; 9:43 for expressions of astonishment.

[3]J. H. Thayer, *Greek-English Lexicon of the New Testament* (Grand Rapids, Mich.: Baker Book House, 1977).

[4]John Galsworthy, *In Chancery and Awakening* (New York: Charles Scribner's Sons, 1969), p. 100.

[5]Ibid.

[6]Jim Reapsome, "Second Career, First Love," *Eternity,* November 1982, p. 25.

[7]Joni Eareckson and Joe Musser, *Joni* (Grand Rapids, Mich.: Zondervan, 1980).

Chapter 10: Job Satisfaction

[1]John Gay and Christopher Pepusch, *The Beggar's Opera,* act 2, sc. 9.

[2]Arthur F. Miller, Jr., and Ralph Mattson, "Find Your Niche" (an interview), *Eternity,* November 1982, p. 21.

[3]Ibid.

[4]Augustine, *Confessions,* trans. R. S. Pine-Coffin (New York: Penguin Classics, 1979), p. 21.

[5]Miller and Mattson, "Find Your Niche," p. 21.

Chapter 11: Church and Career

[1]Diane Dadian, "How to Survive in Your Local Church," *HIS,* June 1983, p. 14.

[2]See Robert V. Thompson, *Unemployed.* (Downers Grove, Ill.: InterVarsity Press, 1983), a helpful booklet for the unemployed Christian who needs perspective. Thompson emphasizes the caring role of the Christian fellowship toward members who are out of work.

[3]Bartlett Hess and Margaret Hess, "A Coping Church," *Eternity,* November 1982, p. 27.